RIBS, RIBS, RIBS

GRILL 'EM · SMOKE 'EM · BAKE 'EM

RIBS, RIBS, RIBS

13-Digit ISBN: 978-1-64643-134-2
10-Digit ISBN: 1-64643-134-0

This book may be ordered by mail from the publisher. Please include $5.99 for postage and handling. Please support your local bookseller first!

Books published by Cider Mill Press Book Publishers are available at special discounts for bulk purchases in the United States by corporations, institutions, and other organizations. For more information, please contact the publisher.

Cider Mill Press Book Publishers
"Where good books are ready for press"
PO Box 454
12 Spring Street
Kennebunkport, Maine 04046

Visit us online
cidermillpress.com

Typography: Sentinel, Bushcraft, Helvetica Rounded
Image Credits: Images on pages 10, 13, 16, 18, 20-21, 22-23, 24, 27, 28-29, 30-31, 33, 35, 40, 44, 46-47, 48, 58, 60, 63, 64, 67, 68, 70, 90, 102, 105, 106, 109, 113, 114, 120-121, 122, 128, 131, 136, 144, 146, 157, 169, 173, 176, 179, 180, 183, 184-185, 186, 189, 190, 192-193, 194, 196-197, 198, 200-201, 203, 204, 206, 209, 210, 213, 215, 216, 219, 225, 226-227, 229, 230, 233, 237, 238, 240-241, 243, 244-245, 246-247, and 249 courtesy of Cider Mill Press Book Publishers LLC. All other images used under official license from Shutterstock.com.

Printed in China
1 2 3 4 5 6 7 8 9 0
First Edition

RIBS, RIBS, RIBS

GRILL 'EM · SMOKE 'EM · BAKE 'EM

CIDER MILL PRESS

BOOK PUBLISHERS

KENNEBUNKPORT, MAINE

Contents

Introduction

Ribs are the holy grail of American barbecue. Whether it's a special holiday meal or a summertime cookout classic, fall-off-the-bone tender ribs are praised and revered everywhere. They're impossible to resist when cooked and seasoned to perfection. Ribs are hard to beat, but if you want to do them right, it takes time and skill. While it might not be overly complicated, there is a certain technique behind preparing perfect ribs. The versatility of ribs lends itself to a multitude of cooking methods and flavor combinations. This book is a collection of the most tantalizing rib recipes that you can enjoy all year long.

Experience the succulent, flavor-packed glory of all things ribs with delicious sides and perfectly paired rubs and marinades. There's nothing like homemade ribs. Once you get over the intimidation factor of cooking ribs, you'll see that they are actually very easy to prepare. With many of the recipes in this book, the active time involved in preparing the meal is about 1 hour. After that, it is about finding the balance between the cut of meat, the temperature, the quality of the smoke, and timing it all just right. If you want to boil the ribs first, grill them, or bake them in the oven, you'll find something to satisfy your cravings in the recipes that follow.

Whether you're a beginner or a grilling master, cooking ribs has never been easier. Fall back on beloved barbecue staples and explore mouth-watering international flavors across a variety of proteins, all supplemented by rubs, seasonings, and sides that will take your meal to new heights. After all, juicy, tender meat is what a meal of ribs is all about, but the meal becomes even better when accompanied with side dishes that complement the seasoning. With *Ribs, Ribs, Ribs* at your side, holiday dinners and backyard barbecues will never be the same again.

Pork Ribs

Pork makes for some of the most flavorful ribs and pairs with seasonings and rubs like no other meat. From the sweetness of brown sugar to the kick of chipotle, the following recipes show why pork ribs are at the heart of barbecue.

Smoked Pork Ribs

YIELD: 4 SERVINGS • ACTIVE TIME: 3 HOURS
TOTAL TIME: 16 HOURS

Any barbecue sauce works well in this recipe, particularly brown sugar or molasses-based sauces.

INGREDIENTS

⅓ cup brown sugar

1 tablespoon chili powder

1 tablespoon smoked paprika

1 tablespoon black pepper

1 tablespoon garlic powder

2 teaspoons kosher salt

1 teaspoon ground cumin

1 (5 lb.) rack pork spareribs, cleaned

2 cups wood chips
(apple wood or cherry wood)

2 cups barbecue sauce of your choosing

2 scallions, sliced on bias (optional)

1 large red chili, seeded and finely diced
(optional)

1 Stir together brown sugar, chili powder, paprika, black pepper, garlic powder, salt, and cumin in a small bowl.

2 Place ribs on a roasting trivet set inside a baking dish lined with aluminum foil. Rub spice mix into ribs, cover dish with foil, and refrigerate overnight.

3 The next day, preheat a charcoal grill or smoker to 250°F. Soak wood chips in a bowl of water.

4 When the coals are lightly covered with ash, place about half the soaked wood chips directly on them. Place ribs on grill, bone side facing down.

5 Cover and cook until very tender, about 3 hours, adding more coals to the grill or smoker as needed to maintain its temperature and generously basting with barbecue sauce; add more wood chips periodically as well.

6 When ribs are ready, remove from grill or smoker and garnish with scallions and chili.

Bourbon Spiked Spareribs

YIELD: 4 SERVINGS • ACTIVE TIME: 30 MINUTES
TOTAL TIME: 1 HOUR AND 30 MINUTES

This is a traditional preparation that hits all the right BBQ notes: sweet up front with a little bite as it goes down.

INGREDIENTS

4 lbs. pork spareribs, trimmed and separated

2 onions, 1 halved, 1 finely diced

2 cloves garlic, 1 halved, 1 crushed

2 tablespoons canola oil

½ cup beef stock

½ orange, juiced

¼ cup ketchup

2 tablespoons soy sauce

2 tablespoons bourbon

1 tablespoon hot mustard

1 tablespoon Worcestershire sauce

1 tablespoon paprika

½ lemon, juiced

1 tablespoon fresh root ginger, peeled and chopped

1 teaspoon kosher salt

½ teaspoon black pepper

1 dash Tabasco™

1 Place ribs in a stock pot and cover with boiling water. Add the halved onion and garlic clove and simmer for 30 minutes.

2 Heat oil in a pan and fry diced onion and the crushed garlic with a pinch of salt for 3 minutes. Stir in broth and orange juice.

3 Cook until slightly reduced and then transfer to a bowl and stir in ketchup, soy sauce, bourbon, mustard, Worcestershire sauce, paprika, lemon juice, ginger, salt, pepper, and Tabasco.

4 Once 30 minutes have passed, remove ribs from the water and pat dry with paper towels.

5 Preheat a gas or charcoal grill to 350°F. Brush ribs with barbecue sauce and grill for 10 to 15 minutes until lightly caramelized, turning ribs and basting with more sauce from time to time.

6 Remove from grill and let rest briefly before serving.

Bourbon Sauce Spareribs

YIELD: 4 SERVINGS • ACTIVE TIME: 30 MINUTES
TOTAL TIME: 10 HOURS

This is another classic approach to ribs, enhanced by the cinnamon in the rub.

INGREDIENTS

For the BBQ sauce

½ cup brown sugar

½ cup unsalted butter, softened

⅓ cup bourbon

¼ cup apple cider vinegar

2 tablespoons Dijon mustard

¼ teaspoon kosher salt

¼ teaspoon black pepper

For the ribs

1 tablespoons kosher salt

1 tablespoon brown sugar

1 teaspoon mustard powder

1 teaspoon dried thyme

1 teaspoon smoked paprika

1 teaspoon ground ginger

1 pinch ground cinnamon

1 (3-lb.) rack pork spareribs, trimmed

3 cloves garlic, crushed

1 tablespoon fresh ginger root, peeled and thinly sliced

2 fresh bay leaves, or 3 dried bay leaves

1½ cups apple cider

1 To begin preparations for the sauce, combine all of the sauce ingredients in a small saucepan and gently warm, whisking until smooth. Remove from heat and set aside to cool.

2 To begin preparations for the ribs, whisk together salt, sugar, mustard powder, thyme, paprika, ginger, and cinnamon in a mixing bowl.

3 Remove membrane from underside of ribs; loosen at ends with a paring knife and pull away by pulling at edges with paper towels in your hands.

4 Rub about 1 tablespoon of seasoning mix into both sides of ribs. Place in a large roasting dish, cover, and refrigerate for at least 6 hours, preferably longer.

5 After chilling, preheat oven or grill to 325°F. Remove ribs from dish and add garlic, ginger, bay leaves, and apple cider to dish, stirring well. Return ribs to dish, meat side facing down, and cover dish with aluminum foil.

6 Bake until meat is tender and coming away from bones, about 2 hours. Remove from oven or grill and let cool, uncovered, for 1 hour.

7 Preheat a gas or charcoal grill to a moderately hot temperature, about 425°F. Grill ribs until lightly charred, turning a few times, about 12 to 15 minutes in total; baste frequently with prepared sauce.

8 Remove ribs when ready and let rest under aluminum foil for at least 10 minutes. Brush with more sauce before cutting ribs between bones.

INGREDIENTS

2 (3-lb.) racks pork spareribs, separated into four pieces

2 cloves garlic, crushed

½ cup tomato paste

⅓ cup ketchup

⅓ cup honey

¼ cup orange juice

¼ cup apple cider vinegar

¼ cup soy sauce

¼ cup bourbon

2 tablespoons Worcestershire sauce

1 teaspoon fresh ginger root, peeled and grated

½ teaspoon black pepper

All-American Spareribs

Orange juice holds this sauce together with the natural sugars and citric tang.

1 Place ribs in a large roasting pan.

2 In a mixing bowl, combine remaining ingredients, stirring until honey dissolves. Pour half over ribs, turning to coat. Cover and refrigerate overnight.

3 The next day, preheat a gas or charcoal grill to 300°F. Place ribs on grill, cover, and cook for 3 hours, turning several times until the ribs are very tender. Remove from grill and increase temperature to 450°F.

4 Return ribs to grill, cooking and basting with remaining sauce until lightly caramelized, about 10 to 15 minutes; turn from time to time.

5 Remove from grill to a platter and serve.

Apple Cider Spareribs

YIELD: 4 SERVINGS • ACTIVE TIME: 1 HOUR
TOTAL TIME: 7 HOURS

The natural sugars in the apple cider are the star of this recipe.

INGREDIENTS

1 (3-lb.) rack pork spareribs, trimmed

3 cups apple cider, plus extra for spraying ribs

2 lemons, juiced

½ cup barbecue dry rub seasoning

1 cup Maple & Bourbon Barbecue Sauce (see page 149)

Fresh cilantro, chopped, for garnish

1 Place ribs in a shallow roasting dish and pour apple cider and lemon juice over ribs, turning several times to coat. Cover and refrigerate for 2 hours.

2 Drain ribs and pat dry with paper towels. Sprinkle dry rub on both sides of the ribs, pressing it into the meat with your fingers. Cover and refrigerate for 2 hours.

3 Preheat a charcoal grill to 300°F. Place ribs on the middle of grill, cover, and cook until meat is tender, about 2½ hours; spray ribs every 30 minutes with apple cider.

4 After 2 hours, lightly brush ribs with barbecue sauce. When the ribs are fully cooked, the meat will be tender enough to pull away from the bone.

5 When ready, remove from grill and let rest under aluminum foil for 10 minutes. Serve with a sprinkle of chopped cilantro.

Sticky Baby Back Ribs

**YIELD: 4 SERVINGS • ACTIVE TIME: 30 MINUTES
TOTAL TIME: 24 HOURS**

Baby back ribs get their name because of how they are butchered. Also known as back ribs, they come from where the ribs connect with a pig's spine, and are shorter than spareribs, hence the diminutive colloquialism. No matter the size, it's a meaty and delicious cut, enhanced here by lime zest and fresh thyme.

INGREDIENTS

Juice of 4 limes

2 tablespoons lime zest

2 red chili peppers, sliced

⅓ cup sugar

¼ cup olive oil

8 fresh thyme sprigs, roughly torn

6 cloves garlic, crushed

1 tablespoon kosher salt

1 teaspoon black pepper

4 lbs. baby back ribs

1 In a mixing bowl, thoroughly stir together lime juice, lime zest, chili peppers, sugar, olive oil, thyme, garlic, salt, and black pepper.

2 Place ribs on a large cutting board, meat side facing down. Remove membrane by loosening at ends with a paring knife and pulling away at edges.

3 Divide ribs between large freezer bags, pouring marinade on top. Expel any excess air from bags before sealing and refrigerate overnight.

4 The next day, preheat oven or grill to 300°F. Remove ribs from marinade and arrange on a roasting trivet set inside a large roasting dish lined with aluminum foil. Pour marinade into a saucepan and cover until needed.

5 Bake ribs until very tender, about 2½ hours. Transfer from the dish to a platter, and cover loosely with aluminum foil.

6 Bring reserved marinade to a boil over a high heat, reducing by about one-half.

7 Preheat broiler or grill to 450°F. Broil or grill ribs until caramelized and lightly charred, turning once, about 6 to 8 minutes in total; baste with reduced marinade from time to time.

8 Transfer to a serving platter and cut into portions.

Texas Baby Back Ribs

YIELD: 4 SERVINGS • ACTIVE TIME: 2 HOURS
TOTAL TIME: 15 HOURS

A simple sauce really puts the meat front and center.

INGREDIENTS

2 tablespoons paprika

½ teaspoon cayenne

2 tablespoons garlic powder

2 teaspoons kosher salt

1 teaspoon black pepper

5 lbs. baby back pork ribs, trimmed

1½ cups ketchup

½ cup hot water

2 tablespoons molasses

1 In a mixing bowl, combine paprika, cayenne, garlic powder, salt, and pepper.

2 Place ribs in a shallow dish and thoroughly apply dry rub to the ribs. Cover and refrigerate for at least 8 hours.

3 After chilling, remove ribs from the fridge. Preheat a gas or charcoal grill to 300°F.

4 Grill ribs for about 2 hours, covered, until meat is tender and pulls away from bones.

5 As the ribs cook, stir together ketchup, water, and molasses in a mixing bowl. Periodically brush ribs with prepared sauce, reserving any sauce that is unused.

6 Remove ribs from grill when ready and let rest under aluminum foil for 10 minutes.

7 Cut ribs into portions to serve. Spoon reserved sauce into individual serving ramekins.

INGREDIENTS

½ cup honey

½ cup ketchup

¼ cup apple cider vinegar, or
distilled white vinegar

2 tablespoons molasses

2 tablespoons bourbon

3 whole star anise, lightly
crushed

4 teaspoons Dijon mustard, or
hot mustard

1 pinch red pepper flakes

3 tablespoons olive oil

2 teaspoons kosher salt

1 teaspoon black pepper

4 lbs. pork spareribs, trimmed

Honey-Roasted Bourbon Spareribs

**YIELD: 4 SERVINGS • ACTIVE TIME: 2 HOURS
TOTAL TIME: 7 TO 24 HOURS**

These ribs get wonderfully caramelized thanks to the sticky sweetness of both honey and molasses.

1 In a mixing bowl combine all ingredients, except the ribs, and stir until honey dissolves.

2 Place ribs on a roasting trivet set inside a large roasting dish lined with aluminum foil. Coat thoroughly in half the marinade and chill for at least 4 hours or overnight.

3 When ready to cook, preheat oven or grill to 300°F.

4 Cook ribs in oven or grill until the meat falls from the bone, about 3 hours; baste with reserved marinade from time to time.

5 When ready, remove ribs and let cool to one side. Preheat broiler or grill to 450°F.

6 Separate ribs and caramelize under broiler or on grill until lightly charred, turning once, about 3 to 5 minutes.

Devil Sauce Spareribs

YIELD: 4 SERVINGS • ACTIVE TIME: 15 MINUTES
TOTAL TIME: 1 HOUR AND 30 MINUTES

The bite of chili peppers, bourbon, vinegar, and Tabasco is undeniable here, but the honey tempers it, resulting in a tangy glaze that still makes pork the star.

INGREDIENTS

2 red chili peppers, seeded and chopped

1 onion, chopped

3 cloves garlic, chopped

1/3 cup honey

2 tablespoons bourbon

1 teaspoon kosher salt

1/2 teaspoon black pepper

1/4 cup tomato paste

1/4 cup red wine vinegar

1 dash Tabasco™

3/4 cup water

4 lbs. pork spareribs, trimmed and separated

Sunflower oil, for brushing

1 In a saucepan, combine chili peppers, onion, garlic, honey, bourbon, salt, black pepper, tomato paste, vinegar, and Tabasco, stirring in water. Bring to a boil over high heat and then reduce to a simmer until smooth and thick, about 10 minutes. Remove from heat and set aside to cool.

2 Preheat a gas or charcoal grill to 350°F. Brush ribs with a little oil and place them on grill, cooking for about 40 minutes, turning occasionally; baste with prepared sauce about 10 minutes before they are ready.

3 Remove from grill and let cool briefly before serving.

Adobo Bourbon Spareribs

YIELD: 4 SERVINGS • ACTIVE TIME: 1 HOUR
TOTAL TIME: 4 HOURS

Using adobo sauce in any dish is an easy and effective way to add smoky heat to food, which makes it ideal for ribs.

INGREDIENTS

2 tablespoons olive oil

1 large yellow onion, chopped

3 cloves garlic, minced

3 tablespoons chopped chipotle chiles in adobo

½ cup red wine vinegar

2 tablespoons fresh lime juice

4 cups tomato sauce

⅓ cup molasses

3 tablespoons bourbon

2 teaspoons mustard powder

2 bay leaves

1 tablespoon kosher salt, plus 1 teaspoon extra

2 (3-lb.) pork sparerib racks, trimmed

2 tablespoons liquid smoke

2 tablespoons brown sugar

2 tablespoons paprika

1 tablespoon chili powder

1 tablespoon black pepper

1 teaspoon cayenne

2 limes, halved

1 Heat oil in a saucepan set over a moderate heat. Add onion and cook until lightly colored, about 5 minutes.

2 Stir in garlic and chiles, cooking for 1 minute. Deglaze pan with vinegar and lime juice, and cook until liquid has reduced by half, 1 to 2 minutes.

3 Stir in adobo sauce, tomato sauce, molasses, bourbon, mustard, bay leaves, and 1 teaspoon salt. Bring to a simmer and cook until thick, stirring occasionally, about 15 to 20 minutes. Remove from heat and strain into a bowl.

4 Place ribs in a stock pot. Cover with water and add the liquid smoke. Bring to a boil over high heat and then reduce to a simmer for 15 minutes. Remove from heat and drain on paper towels.

5 In a bowl, combine the sugar, paprika, chili powder, black pepper, cayenne, and 1 tablespoon salt. Pat ribs with more paper towels before rubbing spice mixture into them.

6 Preheat a gas or charcoal grill to 350°F. Place ribs on grill, cover, and cook for 10 minutes, turning once after 5 minutes. Reduce heat to 300°F.

7 Brush with prepared sauce, cover, and cook for a further 2 hours, or until ribs are very tender.

8 When ready, remove and rest under aluminum foil for 10 minutes. Cut between bones to separate and serve with lime halves on side.

Molasses & Maple Syrup Country Style Pork Ribs

YIELD: 4 SERVINGS • ACTIVE TIME: 25 MINUTES
TOTAL TIME: 2 HOURS

Country-style ribs are a thicker alternative to spareribs, ideal for baking. They can be purchased as separate ribs or in a rack. If you buy a rack, separate ribs before step 1.

INGREDIENTS

3 lbs. bone-in country-style pork ribs

3/4 cup pure maple syrup

1/2 cup ketchup

2 tablespoons lemon juice

1 teaspoon Worcestershire sauce

1/2 teaspoon kosher salt

1/2 teaspoon paprika

1/4 teaspoon ground cinnamon

1/4 teaspoon black pepper

1 pinch cayenne

1 Place ribs in a large stock pot and cover with water. Bring to a boil over high heat and then reduce to a simmer for 10 minutes.

2 Remove from pot and set on paper towels. Pat dry the ribs and then place them in a large oval baking dish and set aside until needed.

3 Preheat oven or grill to 325°F. Whisk together the remaining ingredients in a mixing bowl before pouring over ribs, turning them to coat.

4 Bake until ribs are tender with the meat coming away from the bones, about 1 1/2 to 1 3/4 hours, basting from time to time with sauce.

5 Remove from oven and let stand for 5 minutes before serving.

Lemongrass Spareribs

**YIELD: 4 SERVINGS • ACTIVE TIME: 1 HOUR
TOTAL TIME: 15 HOURS**

That lemony, minty flavor you can't quite put your finger on? It's lemongrass, and it adds a great dynamic to this recipe.

INGREDIENTS

2 cloves garlic, minced

1 small onion, finely chopped

½ cup tomato paste

¼ cup ketchup

⅓ cup honey

⅓ cup orange juice

¼ cup apple cider vinegar

¼ cup soy sauce

2 tablespoons Worcestershire sauce

1 teaspoon fresh ginger root, peeled and finely grated

1 stalk lemongrass, finely chopped

4 lbs. pork spareribs, trimmed

½ cup fresh cilantro, finely chopped

1 In a mixing bowl, combine everything apart from the ribs and cilantro, stirring thoroughly. Divide the marinade in half, reserving one half for dipping or drizzling.

2 Generously brush both sides of the ribs with the remaining marinade, reserving leftover marinade for basting. Cover and refrigerate ribs for at least 12 hours, turning ribs over from time to time.

3 The next day, preheat a gas or charcoal grill to 300°F.

4 Place ribs on center of grill, cover, and cook until meat is tender, about 2 hours; about 20-30 minutes before serving, brush with remaining marinade.

5 Transfer ribs to a cutting board and let rest under aluminum foil for 10 minutes before cutting into individual or 2-rib sections.

6 Scatter with chopped cilantro before serving.

Teriyaki Pork Ribs

YIELD: 4 SERVINGS • ACTIVE TIME: 30 MINUTES
TOTAL TIME: 2 HOURS AND 30 MINUTES

American-style barbecue sauces rely heavily on ketchup. Using a sauce that isn't built around tomato takes ribs to a whole other level.

INGREDIENTS

For the ribs

1 (4-lb.) rack pork spareribs, trimmed

1 tablespoon brown sugar

1 teaspoon kosher salt

¼ teaspoon black pepper

2 teaspoons sesame oil

For the glaze

1 tablespoon canola oil

4 whole star anise

1 tablespoon peeled and minced fresh ginger root

1 clove garlic, finely chopped

3 red chilies, finely sliced

¼ cup honey

3 tablespoons soy sauce

1½ tablespoons rice vinegar

1 teaspoon sesame oil

1 teaspoon cornstarch, mixed to a slurry with 2 tablespoons water

1 small handful fresh cilantro, torn

1 To begin preparation for the ribs, preheat the oven or grill to 325°F. Place ribs on a roasting trivet set inside a large roasting dish lined with aluminum foil.

2 Stir together sugar, salt, black pepper, and sesame oil in a small bowl. Rub mixture all over ribs.

3 Bake in the oven or grill until ribs are golden-brown and tender, about 2 hours.

4 As the ribs cook, begin preparation for the glaze. Heat canola oil in a saucepan set over medium heat. Stir in the star anise, frying for 30 seconds until fragrant. Add ginger, garlic, and chilies, cooking and stirring until fragrant, about 2 minutes. Stir in honey, soy sauce, vinegar, and sesame oil.

5 Bring to a boil and then whisk in cornstarch slurry, cooking until slightly thickened and reduced, about 2 to 4 minutes. Set aside.

6 Remove ribs from oven or grill when ready. Preheat broiler or grill to 425°F.

7 Brush ribs with half of glaze, cooking under broiler or on grill until sticky and lightly caramelized, about 10 to 15 minutes; baste with remaining glaze from time to time.

8 Remove and let stand briefly before serving with a garnish of cilantro.

Chinese-Style Pork Ribs

YIELD: 4 SERVINGS • ACTIVE TIME: 10 MINUTES
TOTAL TIME: 1 HOUR

Not as sweet as balsamic vinegar, Chinese black vinegar is made from glutinous rice and malt, which imparts a complex fruity quality to the flavor, and to these ribs.

INGREDIENTS

3 lbs. pork ribs, trimmed and separated

1 shallot, finely chopped

¼ cup canola oil

2 cloves garlic, finely chopped

3 tablespoons fresh ginger root, peeled and finely chopped

¼ cup brown sugar

¼ cup maple syrup

⅓ cup rice wine

⅓ cup Chinese black vinegar

½ cup light soy sauce

1 Place ribs in a large pot and cover with water. Bring to a boil and then simmer for 20 minutes.

2 Pour oil into saucepan over medium heat and add the shallot, frying for 5 to 8 minutes. Stir in garlic and ginger and fry for a few minutes.

3 Stir in sugar, maple syrup, rice wine, vinegar, and soy sauce. Bring to a simmer, cooking until reduced and thickened.

4 Once 20 minutes have passed, drain ribs and let cool, patting dry with paper towels.

5 Preheat a gas or charcoal grill to 325°F. Place ribs on grill and cook until meat is very tender and lightly charred all over, about 15 to 20 minutes; baste with reduced sauce every 2 to 3 minutes.

6 When ready to serve, transfer to a platter and brush with remaining sauce before serving.

Korean-Style Pork Ribs

YIELD: 4 SERVINGS • ACTIVE TIME: 30 MINUTES
TOTAL TIME: 7 HOURS

There is impressive depth to the soy-sweet flavoring in play here, and there is nothing spicy about it for those adverse to such things.

1 Place ribs in one layer in a shallow dish. Mix together garlic, soy sauce, honey, hoisin, vinegar, and rice wine and pour over the ribs, coating well. Cover and refrigerate for at least 6 hours.

2 Preheat oven or grill to 350°F.

3 Transfer ribs and marinade to a roasting dish and cook until golden-brown and tender, about 35 to 45 minutes; brush with marinade from time to time and turn ribs once or twice.

4 Remove and let stand briefly before serving with a sprinkle of sesame seeds and some cilantro.

INGREDIENTS

4 lbs. pork spareribs, trimmed

2 cloves garlic, finely chopped

½ cup soy sauce

¼ cup honey

2 tablespoons hoisin sauce

2 tablespoons rice vinegar

2 tablespoons rice wine

2 tablespoons sesame seeds

Fresh cilantro, to garnish

Rosemary Spareribs

YIELD: 4 SERVINGS • ACTIVE TIME: 30 MINUTES
TOTAL TIME: 4 HOURS AND 30 MINUTES

The woodsy, lemon-pine flavor of rosemary goes perfectly with the ribs in this preparation.

INGREDIENTS

4½ lbs. pork spareribs, trimmed

3 cloves garlic, minced

½ cup olive oil

Kosher salt, to taste

Black pepper, to taste

4 sprigs fresh rosemary, plus extra to garnish

1 Separate ribs into individual servings (3 to 4 ribs per serving). Place ribs in a large roasting dish.

2 In a small bowl, mix garlic, olive oil, salt, and pepper. Pour marinade over ribs, coating the ribs completely. Lay rosemary sprigs on the meat.

3 Cover and refrigerate for at least 2 hours, preferably longer.

4 When ready to cook, preheat a gas or charcoal grill to 325°F. Discard rosemary sprigs, place ribs on grill, and cook for 2 hours, or until meat is tender.

5 Remove from grill and let rest under aluminum foil for 10 minutes before serving with a garnish of rosemary.

INGREDIENTS

2 tablespoons unsalted butter

1 small pineapple, peeled, cored, and diced

1 cup low-sodium soy sauce

½ cup bourbon

½ cups ketchup

3 tablespoons apple cider vinegar

¼ cup brown sugar

1 tablespoon red pepper flakes

2 cloves garlic, chopped

1 tablespoon fresh ginger root, peeled and grated

3 lbs. baby back pork ribs, trimmed

2 tablespoons toasted sesame oil

Kosher salt, to taste

Black pepper, to taste

¾ cup sesame seeds

Sesame Crusted Pork Ribs

YIELD: 4 SERVINGS • ACTIVE TIME: 30 MINUTES
TOTAL TIME: 3 HOURS AND 30 MINUTES

Sweet pineapple plays well here with the nuttiness of sesame seed.

1 Preheat oven or grill to 300°F.

2 In a saucepan over medium heat, melt butter and add the pineapple chunks, sautéing for 3 minutes.

3 Stir in soy sauce, bourbon, ketchup, vinegar, brown sugar, red pepper, garlic, and ginger. Bring to a slow simmer and cook, stirring, until thickened, about 20 minutes.

4 Pour glaze into a blender and purée until smooth. Set aside.

5 Place ribs on a roasting trivet set inside a large roasting dish and rub all over with sesame oil. Season generously with salt and pepper.

6 Roast until meat is tender and coming away from bones, about 3 hours; baste with glaze for remaining 30 minutes of cooking.

7 Remove ribs when ready and baste with any remaining glaze before generously sprinkling with sesame seeds. Preheat broiler or grill to 450°F.

8 Cook under broiler or on grill until sesame seeds are golden-brown, about 5 to 7 minutes.

9 Cut between bones to separate before serving.

Spicy Oyster Sauce Pork Ribs

YIELD: 4 SERVINGS • ACTIVE TIME: 15 MINUTES
TOTAL TIME: 5 HOURS AND 40 MINUTES

If you're not a fan of oysters, don't be put off by oyster sauce. Yes, it is made from caramelized oyster juice, but this flavor enhancer isn't fishy or briny. It has a sweet-savory tang that evokes soy sauce and barbecue sauce, which is why it works so well in this recipe.

INGREDIENTS

2 cloves garlic, finely chopped

1 tablespoon fresh ginger root, peeled and finely chopped

1 lime, juiced

⅓ cup oyster sauce

¼ cup soy sauce

1 teaspoon red pepper flakes

1 teaspoon ground cumin

½ teaspoon ground coriander

3 tablespoons brown sugar

2 tablespoons olive oil

2 tablespoons sesame oil

3 tablespoons water

½ teaspoon kosher salt

¼ teaspoon black pepper

4 lbs. pork spareribs, trimmed and separated

3 scallions, sliced

1 red chili, finely sliced

1 small bunch fresh cilantro, roughly chopped

1 lime, cut into wedges

1 In a shallow dish, mix together everything for the marinade, except for the ribs. Place ribs in the marinade, turning to coat. Cover and refrigerate for 4 hours.

2 When you are ready to cook the ribs, remove them from the fridge and preheat a gas or charcoal grill to 325°F.

3 Cook ribs until they are tender and nicely colored, turning a few times, about 1 hour; baste with marinade from time to time.

4 To serve, arrange ribs on a serving plate or dish and scatter over scallions, chili, and cilantro. Serve with wedges of lime on side.

Asian Spareribs

YIELD: 4 SERVINGS • ACTIVE TIME: 20 MINUTES
TOTAL TIME: 24 HOURS

St. Louis-style spareribs are ideal for this recipe that features a spicy and flowery depth of flavor.

1 Whisk together everything apart from the ribs in a mixing bowl until sugar and honey have dissolved.

2 Place ribs in a large freezer bag; if too large, cut rack in half and place in two separate bags.

3 Pour about two-thirds of the sauce into the bag(s), expelling any excess air before sealing and chilling overnight. Cover and reserve remaining sauce.

4 The next day, preheat oven or grill to 275°F. Line a large roasting dish with aluminum foil and sit a large roasting trivet on top.

5 Remove ribs from bag(s) and arrange on trivet. Bake until ribs are very tender, about 2 hours and 30 minutes; baste with reserved sauce from time to time.

6 Remove ribs and let rest under aluminum foil for 10 minutes. Preheat broiler or grill to 450°F.

7 Caramelize ribs under broiler or on grill, turning once, until golden-brown and sticky, about 6 to 8 minutes in total.

8 Remove and let cool briefly before cutting and serving.

INGREDIENTS

¾ cup hoisin sauce

⅓ cup dark soy sauce

3 tablespoons brown sugar

3 tablespoons honey

1 tablespoon sesame oil

1 tablespoon Chinese five-spice powder

1 teaspoon onion powder

1 teaspoon garlic powder

1 teaspoon ground ginger

1 (4-lb.) rack pork spareribs, cleaned and trimmed

Hoisin Spareribs

YIELD: 4 SERVINGS • ACTIVE TIME: 20 MINUTES
TOTAL TIME: 24 HOURS

The hoisin sauce gives these spareribs a wonderfully vibrant flavor.

INGREDIENTS

1 (3-lb.) rack pork spareribs, trimmed

2 cups white sugar

²/₃ cup ketchup

¼ cup Shaoxing wine, Chinese cooking wine

¼ cup dark soy sauce

¼ cup hoisin sauce

1 tablespoon kosher salt

1 teaspoon freshly ground white pepper

1 teaspoon Chinese five-spice powder

1 teaspoon ground ginger

1 handful fresh cilantro, torn

1 Place ribs in a large freezer bag; if too large, cut rack in half and place in two separate bags.

2 In a mixing bowl, whisk together the remaining ingredients, apart from cilantro, until a gritty sauce forms.

3 Pour about half of the sauce into bag(s), expelling any excess air before sealing and refrigerating overnight. Cover and reserve remaining sauce.

4 The next day, preheat oven or grill to 300°F. Line a large roasting dish with aluminum foil and sit a large roasting trivet on top.

5 Remove ribs from bag(s) and arrange on trivet. Bake until meat is very tender, about 2¹/₂ hours; baste with reserved sauce from time to time.

6 Remove ribs when ready and let rest under aluminum foil for at least 10 minutes. Preheat broiler or grill to 450°F.

7 Cut between bones to separate into ribs. Broil until lightly charred and caramelized, turning once halfway through, about 6 to 8 minutes in total.

8 Transfer ribs to a platter and garnish with cilantro.

INGREDIENTS

For the ribs

6 cloves garlic, minced

3 tablespoons brown sugar

3 tablespoons balsamic vinegar

½ teaspoon cayenne

1 tablespoon kosher salt

1 teaspoon black pepper

1 (4-lb.) rack pork spareribs, cleaned and trimmed

½ cup water

For the glaze

½ cup balsamic vinegar

1 cups hot water

¼ cups brown sugar, packed

¼ cups ketchup

1 tablespoon molasses

½ teaspoon mustard powder

Balsamic Pork Ribs

YIELD: 4 SERVINGS • ACTIVE TIME: 20 MINUTES
TOTAL TIME: 24 HOURS

This recipe is perfect for summertime grilling. The brown sugar and balsamic glaze caramelizes the edges of these ribs and is given a touch of smokiness over the grill.

1 To begin preparations for the ribs, stir together garlic, sugar, vinegar, cayenne, salt, and pepper in a mixing bowl.

2 Rub marinade into both sides of ribs. Place ribs in a large roasting dish and cover dish with aluminum foil. Refrigerate overnight.

3 The next day, preheat oven or grill to 425°F. Pour water into dish around ribs and cover with foil.

4 Roast until ribs are tender, about 2 hours. Remove and transfer ribs to a platter.

5 To begin preparations for the glaze, whisk together everything for the glaze in a saucepan and pour any juices from the roasting dish into the saucepan.

6 Bring glaze to a boil over medium heat, whisking from time to time. Cook until glaze has reduced and thickened, about 8 to 10 minutes.

7 Preheat broiler or grill to 450°F. Brush ribs with glaze before caramelizing under broiler, or on grill, until golden-brown and sticky, turning once, about 6 to 8 minutes in total.

8 Transfer to a platter and cut into portions, serving with remaining glaze on side.

Basic Grilled Double-Cut Rib Chops

**YIELD: 4 TO 6 SERVINGS • ACTIVE TIME: 25 MINUTES
TOTAL TIME: 45 MINUTES**

Properly cooked, a great chop will burst with flavor. With this dish, there's no need to overpower the pork. Just sprinkle the chops with a hint of salt and fresh cracked pepper.

INGREDIENTS

4-6 double-cut pork rib chops

Sea salt, to taste

Black pepper, to taste

1 Preheat one side of your grill to 400°F. If possible, create a two-zone cooking area: one zone will be your hot zone, concentrating your coals or heat source beneath one side of your grilling area, while the second zone will be arranged on the opposite side of the grill with little to no coals or flame beneath this surface area. Use the hot side to wear your chops, and the cool side to allow your chops to cook through the radiating heat. This will help ensure that your chops do not overcook and dry out.

2 Place the chops directly over the hot zone and sear both sides of the chops until evenly browned, about 5 minutes perside. Keep a watchful eye on the grill during this stage, as fat drippings can create flare-ups that will char rather than sear the meat.

3 Once the chops are seared golden brown, move them over to the cooler zone and let them cook more thoroughly and slowly. If using a meat probe thermometer, look for 135°F for medium-rare and approximately 145°F for a tender and flavorful medium. Season with salt and pepper.

INGREDIENTS

4-5 sparerib pork chops

All-purpose flour, as needed

2 tablespoons clarified butter

3 tablespoons olive oil

¾ cup red wine

Salt and pepper, to taste

2¾ cups blueberries

½ cup honey

Blueberry Pork Chops

**YIELD: 4 SERVINGS • ACTIVE TIME: 1 HOUR AND 20 MINUTES
TOTAL TIME: 2 HOURS**

Pork goes so well with sweet fruits, and blueberries are no exception!

1 Get your grill started, shooting for a temperature of about 375 to 400°F. Meanwhile, dust your chops with flour.

2 Melt the clarified butter and olive oil in a saucepan that can withstand the flames of your grill. Add the pork chops and cook over the grill until evenly browned.

3 Add the wine and cook off the alcohol and reduce the wine so it becomes a flavorful stock, adding salt and pepper to your preferred taste.

4 Mix the blueberries and the honey in a food blender, one that will allow you to easily spatula off the blueberry-honey concoction from the bottom and sides of the blender. A food processor works wonders in this situation as it has a nice wide opening.

5 Coat the pork chops with the blueberry-honey mixture and grill them over the open flame to sear in the final flavors, about 5 minutes per side.

6 As the chops have already cooked in the saucepan, they should not need more than a minute or two on each side before being ready to serve. Try to let your chops stand for about 10 minutes before serving.

Killer BBQ Spareribs

YIELD: 6 TO 8 SERVINGS • ACTIVE TIME: 1 HOUR AND 45 MINUTES • TOTAL TIME: 4 TO 5 HOURS

INGREDIENTS

2-3 cloves of garlic, sliced extra thin

1 clove garlic, crushed or minced

1 cup honey

⅓ cup dark molasses

⅓ cup local dark maple syrup

1½ tablespoons paprika

1 teaspoon sea salt

1½ teaspoons freshly ground pepper

1 tablespoon chili ancho powder (add more if you like your BBQ extra spicy)

2 teaspoons ground cumin

½ cup apple cider vinegar (the more you add, the tangier the flavor)

1½ cups organic strained tomatoes

5-6 oz. organic tomato paste (no sugar added)

¼ cup chili sauce

¼ cup Worcestershire sauce

1½ tablespoons fresh lemon juice

5 tablespoons chopped onions

1 teaspoon mustard powder

½ pineapple, cubed (if fresh juice collects on your cutting board, add that in, too!)

4-5 lbs. pork spareribs

Without approaching the task via a day-long, low-heat smoking process, tackle your ribs a little bit more conventionally (and much more simply). First, slow roast the ribs in the oven at a low temperature of 200°F for about 3 hours. This allows the acids and seasonings to gently tenderize the meat, while the low heat loosens the meat from the bone so the cooked rib meat will pull away without fuss. Use a covered turkey roasting pan. The cover keeps the moisture inside the roasting pan, which helps the seasoning seep into the meat and tenderizes, too. And the pan is long enough to keep the full rack of ribs intact for easier grilling.

1 Preheat the oven to 325°F. Meanwhile, mix all of the ingredients except the ribs themselves in a large sauce pan over low to medium heat and allow the sugars to melt. Line the bottom of the roasting pan with a thick layer of the BBQ sauce.

2 Place each rack of ribs into the roasting pan, layering them with a solid basting of the sauce so both sides of each rack of ribs are fully coated. Cover and allow the ribs to cook for 2½ to 3 hours. No need to turn or recoat the ribs during this process.

3 About 15 to 20 minutes before the ribs have finished cooking in your oven, fire up your grill to medium heat.

4 Use long tongs that will allow you to slide the tong the full length of the rack of ribs. This will help prevent the ribs from breaking off, as the ribs will be soft and tender from their time in the oven.

5 As soon as the flames char an edge of the meat, quickly baste over that area with a fresh coat of sauce and turn the ribs so the opposite side can be lightly and evenly seared by the fire as well. Unlike steaks on the grill, turn the ribs over and over, basting and turning each rack in order to achieve the best and most flavorful results. Don't worry about a little bit of blackening and charring; paint over all the charred areas with a fresh coat of BBQ sauce and the two flavors wed together beautifully.

6 As soon as the ribs reach the level of browning and blackening you desire, remove the ribs from the grill and place them onto a serving tray. Do not place them back into the roasting pan. Bring the ribs directly to the table and allow them to cool before digging in.

> **TIP:** THE MORE LAYERS OF SAUCE, THE RICHER THE TASTE.

Beef & Lamb Ribs

The versatility of beef lends itself to almost any flavor combination, and the naturally outstanding taste of lamb pairs nicely with a refreshing mint or citrus. The following recipes highlight the best of both beef and lamb ribs.

Beef Ribs with Bourbon BBQ Sauce

YIELD: 4 SERVINGS • ACTIVE TIME: 1 HOUR
TOTAL TIME: 16 HOURS

This recipe is everything ribs should be—mouth-watering, juicy, and melt-in-your-mouth delicious.

1 To begin preparations for the ribs, stir together sugar, salt, paprika, black pepper, mustard powder, and cayenne in a mixing bowl.

2 Rub the spice mix into both sides of the ribs. Divide ribs between two large roasting dishes, covering them with aluminum foil. Refrigerate overnight.

3 The next day, preheat the oven or grill to 325°F. Pour 2 cups of the stock into each dish around the ribs and re-cover with foil.

4 Bake in the oven or grill until beef is very tender, about 3 hours. When ready, transfer to platters and cover loosely with aluminum foil. Preheat broiler or grill to 450°F.

5 To begin preparations for the sauce, combine all ingredients in a small saucepan. Bring to a simmer, whisking until sugar dissolves.

6 Let simmer until slightly thickened, about 3 to 5 minutes. Remove from heat and let cool for 10 minutes.

7 Brush some sauce onto ribs. Place ribs under broiler or on grill, cooking until caramelized and lightly charred, turning once, about 6 to 8 minutes; baste with more sauce from time to time.

8 Transfer to a platter and cut between bones into ribs before serving.

INGREDIENTS

For the ribs

2 tablespoons brown sugar

2 teaspoons kosher salt

2 teaspoons smoked paprika

1 teaspoon black pepper

½ teaspoon mustard powder

1 pinch cayenne

5 lbs. beef short ribs, cleaned and trimmed

4 cups beef stock, divided

For the sauce

¾ cup brown sugar

1 cup ketchup

¼ cup red wine vinegar or apple cider vinegar

1 tablespoon water

1 tablespoon bourbon

1 teaspoon tomato paste

1 teaspoon Worcestershire sauce

1 tablespoon mustard powder

1 teaspoon paprika

1 teaspoon kosher salt

½ teaspoon black pepper

INGREDIENTS

For the ribs

¼ cup bourbon

2 tablespoons brown sugar

2 teaspoons kosher salt

2 teaspoons smoked paprika

1 teaspoon black pepper

1 pinch cayenne

5 lbs. beef short ribs, trimmed

4 cups beef stock, divided

For the glaze

1 cup stock

¼ cup brown sugar

¼ cup bourbon

Bourbon Glazed Beef Short Ribs

**YIELD: 4 SERVINGS • ACTIVE TIME: 20 MINUTES
TOTAL TIME: 24 HOURS**

Look for beef short rib racks, rather than whole ribs, for the best results.

1 To begin preparations for the ribs, stir together bourbon, sugar, salt, paprika, black pepper, and cayenne in a mixing bowl.

2 Place ribs on a large cutting board, meat side facing down. Remove membrane by loosening at ends with a paring knife and pulling away at edges with paper towels in your hands.

3 Rub the marinade into both sides of ribs. Divide ribs between two large roasting dishes, covering them with aluminum foil. Chill overnight.

4 The next day, preheat oven or grill to 325°F. Pour 2 cups of broth into each dish around ribs and re-cover with foil.

5 Bake in oven or grill until beef is very tender, about 2 1/2 to 3 hours. When ready, transfer to platters and cover loosely with aluminum foil. Preheat broiler or grill to 450°F.

6 To begin preparations for the glaze, whisk together broth, sugar, and bourbon in a saucepan. Bring to a boil over a medium heat and cook until reduced by half, about 10 minutes.

7 Brush some glaze onto ribs. Place ribs under broiler or on grill, grilling until caramelized and lightly charred, turning once, about 6-8 minutes; baste with more glaze from time to time.

8 Transfer to a platter and cut racks into ribs before serving.

Grilled Beef Ribs

**YIELD: 4 SERVINGS • ACTIVE TIME: 20 MINUTES
TOTAL TIME: 1 HOUR AND 30 MINUTES**

Boiling the ribs first helps jump-start the cooking process.

INGREDIENTS

5 lbs. beef whole ribs, trimmed and separated

2 red chili peppers, finely chopped

1 onion, diced

2 garlic cloves, roughly chopped

¼ cup honey

1 teaspoon salt

½ teaspoon black pepper

4 tablespoons tomato paste

2 tablespoons white wine vinegar

1 dash Tabasco™

¾ cup water

Canola oil, for brushing

1 Place ribs in a stock pot of boiling water and reduce to a simmer for 20 minutes. Drain and pat dry with paper towels.

2 In a saucepan, mix together chili peppers, onion, garlic, honey, salt, black pepper, tomato paste, vinegar, and Tabasco in a saucepan. Whisk in water and bring to a boil. Cook for 10 minutes until reduced and thickened. Remove from heat and leave to cool.

3 Preheat gas or charcoal grill to 350°F.

4 Brush ribs with oil and grill for 20 minutes, turning once and occasionally basting with the prepared sauce.

5 Remove from grill and let rest under aluminum foil for 10 minutes before serving.

INGREDIENTS

½ cup brown sugar

½ cup soy sauce

¼ cup bourbon

¼ cup olive oil

3 cloves garlic, minced

2 tablespoons fresh ginger
root, peeled and grated

4 lbs. beef short ribs, trimmed
and separated

2 large sweet onions, sliced
into ½-inch rounds and
speared with toothpicks

Grilled Bourbon Short Ribs with Onions

YIELD: 4 SERVINGS • ACTIVE TIME: 30 MINUTES
TOTAL TIME: 3 HOURS

This is a homey dish that tastes especially good when autumn arrives. Don't skip the onions—when grilled and flavored with the sauce they take on a wonderful charred sweetness.

1 In a mixing bowl, combine sugar, soy sauce, bourbon, olive oil, garlic, and ginger. Place ribs in a large resealable plastic freezer bag.

2 Pour the two-thirds of the marinade over ribs and securely seal the bag, expelling any excess air. Turn bag over several times to completely coat ribs. Refrigerate for at least 2 hours, preferably longer. Cover and refrigerate remaining marinade.

3 When ready to cook the ribs, preheat a gas or charcoal grill to 375°F.

4 Remove ribs from marinade and place on grill, grilling for 15 to 20 minutes until tender and cooked through, turning once after 10 minutes; brush with reserved marinade from time to time.

5 Remove from grill and let rest under aluminum foil.

6 Place onions on grill and cook until lightly charred, also brushing with marinade from time to time, about 7 to 10 minutes.

7 Remove from grill, transfer to a platter, and remove toothpicks before arranging ribs on top and serving.

Caribbean Beef Ribs

YIELD: 4 SERVINGS • ACTIVE TIME: 30 MINUTES
TOTAL TIME: 18 HOURS

The pungent sweet and smoky spices in this dry rub impart an island flair that is enlivened when you finish off these ribs with a healthy squeeze of lime juice.

INGREDIENTS

1 (4-lb.) rack beef whole ribs, trimmed

2 tablespoons brown sugar

2 tablespoons onion powder

2 tablespoons garlic powder

1 tablespoon kosher salt

1 tablespoon smoked paprika, or regular paprika

2 teaspoons cayenne

2 teaspoons ground allspice

2 teaspoons black pepper

1 teaspoon red pepper flakes

1 teaspoon ground cumin

1 teaspoon ground nutmeg

1 teaspoon ground cinnamon

1 teaspoon dried thyme

2 limes, halved

1 Stir together all the ingredients, except the ribs and limes, in a small bowl.

2 Rub the seasoning mix into both sides of the ribs. Place the ribs on a roasting trivet set inside a large roasting pan lined with aluminum foil. Cover and refrigerate overnight.

3 The next day, preheat an oven or grill to 275°F.

4 Roast the ribs until very tender, about 6 hours. The ribs are done when the meat is falling away from the bones.

5 Remove the ribs from the oven or grill and let rest under aluminium foil for 10 minutes.

6 Cut between the bones into the ribs and arrange on a dish, serving with the lime halves.

Grilled Sesame Seed Beef Ribs

YIELD: 4 SERVINGS • ACTIVE TIME: 20 MINUTES
TOTAL TIME: 6 HOURS AND 30 MINUTES

Whole ribs are longer and thinner compared to short ribs, although short ribs would also work in this recipe.

1 Preheat oven or grill to 275°F. Place ribs on a large cutting board, meat side facing down. Remove membrane by loosening at ends with a paring knife and pulling away at edges with paper towels in your hands.

2 Stir together hoisin sauce, honey, vinegar, salt, and pepper in a mixing bowl. Rub about half the sauce all over the ribs and then place them on a roasting trivet set inside a large roasting dish lined with aluminum foil.

3 Bake until very tender, between 5 and 6 hours, basting from time to time with the remaining sauce; when ready, the meat should be falling away from the bones.

4 Remove from oven or grill and let rest under aluminum foil for 10 minutes.

5 Cut between bones into ribs and arrange in a serving dish, garnished with sesame seeds, scallions, chili, and cilantro. Serve with the lemon wedges.

INGREDIENTS

1 (3-lb.) rack whole beef ribs, trimmed

1 cup hoisin sauce

2 tablespoons honey

1 tablespoon rice vinegar

½ teaspoon kosher salt

½ teaspoon black pepper

2 tablespoons sesame seeds

2 scallions, finely sliced

2 red chilies, seeded and finely sliced

1 handful fresh cilantro, torn

1 lemon, cut into wedges

Kalbi

**YIELD: 4 SERVINGS • ACTIVE TIME: 30 MINUTES
TOTAL TIME: 5 HOURS**

Korean-style short ribs can be sourced from most good Asian markets. They may also be labeled as flanken ribs; these ribs are easy to identify as they are butchered across the rib bones, meaning each slice has a few pieces of bone. The sweet and savory marinade is elevated by the gochujang, a fermented spice paste, making for tender and tasty beef.

1 Place ribs on a large cutting board and sprinkle with sugar, rubbing sugar into ribs. Let stand at room temperature for 10 minutes.

2 In a mixing bowl whisk together soy sauce, water, mirin, gochujang, onion, garlic, ginger, and sesame oil.

3 Transfer ribs to a large shallow dish and pour over marinade, turning ribs to coat. Cover and refrigerate for at least 4 hours, preferably longer; turn ribs over every 2 hours.

4 When ready to cook, preheat a gas or charcoal grill to 400°F; if using a charcoal grill, wait until the coals turn white hot.

5 Remove ribs from marinade, wiping off excess with paper towels. Lay onto grill, cooking until charred and browned all over, turning once, about 6 to 8 minutes in total.

6 Remove from grill and let rest under aluminum foil for 10 minutes before slicing and serving.

INGREDIENTS

5 lbs. beef short ribs, Korean-style

1 cup brown sugar

1 cup soy sauce

$\frac{1}{3}$ cup water

$\frac{1}{3}$ cup mirin

2 tablespoons gochujang

1 small onion, grated

5 cloves garlic, minced

1 tablespoon fresh ginger root, peeled and minced

$1\frac{1}{2}$ tablespoons toasted sesame oil

Perfect Prime Rib

YIELD: 6 TO 7 SERVINGS • ACTIVE TIME: 1 HOUR
TOTAL TIME: 5 HOURS

Prime rib takes center stage during the holiday season, and for very good reason. Fortunately, it's also very easy to cook.

1 Remove the rib roast from the refrigerator 30 minutes before cooking and let stand at room temperature. Preheat the oven to 450°F.

2 Generously apply the garlic paste onto the meat side and both ends of the prime rib, followed by half the sea salt and pepper.

3 Chop 1 bunch of rosemary and 1 bunch of thyme and place in a small bowl. Mix with the rest of the salt and pepper. Press the herb mixture against the side of the meat so it sticks.

4 Place a roasting rack in the center of a roasting pan. Take the remaining rosemary and thyme bunches and set on the rack so that they form a bed, alternating the rosemary and thyme.

5 Place the roast meat-side down onto the herb-covered rack.

6 Place the roast in the oven and cook for 20 minutes, and lower the temperature to 325°F. Cook the roast for about 3 to 4 more hours until internal temperature reaches 130°F.

7 Remove the roast from the oven, transfer to a large carving board, and let stand for about 15 minutes before carving.

INGREDIENTS

1 (6-rib) rib roast
with ribs removed

5 medium garlic cloves,
crushed into a fine paste

3 tablespoons sea salt,
coarse if possible

4 tablespoons coarsely
ground black pepper

6 bunches fresh rosemary

6 bunches fresh thyme

Prime Rib au Poivre

YIELD: 4 SERVINGS • ACTIVE TIME: 1 HOUR AND 30 MINUTES
TOTAL TIME: 4 HOURS

INGREDIENTS

1 (6-rib) rib roast

3 medium garlic cloves, finely chopped

2 tablespoons Dijon mustard

3 to 4 tablespoons whole black peppercorns

1 tablespoon sea salt

3 bunches fresh rosemary (optional)

The au poivre works well when served on select red meats. You can find a Filet Mignon au Poivre at nearly every steakhouse. The au poivre style simply requires you to heavily pepper your meat so that its sharp, spicy flavors enter the meat at a shallow level. Likewise, because the flavors are so heavy and powerful, the au poivre style works perfectly on meats that have a relatively small surface area, such as the filet mignon or prime rib. The cap of the prime rib, or the fatty outer rim of the rib roast, is easily permeated with flavor that goes perfectly with the au poivre technique. To add a little bit of a flair to this recipe, add a Dijon-garlic paste as a base layer to the au poivre to broaden the flavors.

1 Remove the rib roast from the refrigerator 1 hour before cooking and let stand at room temperature.

2 Preheat the oven to 325°F.

3 Mix the garlic and Dijon mustard in a small bowl so that it forms a paste. When the meat is at room temperature, generously apply the paste to the meat side of the prime rib. Use your hands so that the mustard will spread into the prime rib's cap.

4 Place the whole black peppercorns in a small, sealable bag and seal tightly. Place the bag on a flat surface and then, using the bottom of a heavy pan such as a cast-iron skillet, firmly pound the peppercorns so that they split into large pieces—much more coarse than what a traditional pepper mill will give you. Remove the split peppercorns from the bag and mix in a small bowl with the sea salt.

5 Using your hands, generously pat the split peppercorns and sea salt onto the prime rib already rubbed with the Dijon-garlic paste. If desired, divide the bunches of rosemary evenly and place in between the ribs; tie firmly with butcher's twine so that the rosemary stays in place while roasting.

6 Transfer the au poivre prime rib onto a large rack set in a roasting pan. Transfer the rib roast to the oven and cook for 2½ to 3 hours, until a thermometer registers 125°F for medium-rare. During the roasting process, the crust of the rib roast may begin to brown; if so, gently cover it with a sheet of aluminum foil in order to help maintain the moisture of the crust.

7 Remove the rib roast from the oven, transfer to a large carving board, and let stand for about 10 minutes before carving.

TIP: YOU CAN USE THE JUICES LEFT OVER IN THE ROASTING PAN FOR AN AU JUS, IF YOU LIKE IT VERY PEPPERY. IN THAT CASE, DOUBLE THE AMOUNT OF RED WINE AND BEEF BROTH USED IN THE RECIPE, MAINTAINING A 1:2 RATIO.

Rotisserie-Grilled Prime Rib

YIELD: 6 TO 8 SERVINGS • ACTIVE TIME: 1 HOUR AND 15 MINUTES • TOTAL TIME: 4 HOURS

The rotisserie is a great tool on a summer evening for a quick prime rib. One of my favorite elements to this meal is that its timing is extremely easy: only 16 to 18 minutes per pound of meat. When you rotisserie the meat, the constant, slow turning of the meat ensures it will receive equal amounts of heat, which quickens the cooking process. Be sure to place an aluminum pan under the rib roast as it is cooking to catch the juices that will fall out; they can be used for a basic au jus.

INGREDIENTS

1 (6-rib) rib roast

3 tablespoons extra-virgin olive oil

4 garlic cloves, minced

1 small shallot, finely chopped

2 tablespoons coarse sea salt

2 tablespoons coarsely ground black pepper

3 bunches fresh thyme

3 bunches fresh rosemary

2 cups hickory or maple wood chips

1 Rub the rib roast with 1 tablespoon of the extra-virgin olive oil and let rest at room temperature for 1 hour.

2 In a small bowl, combine the minced garlic and finely chopped shallot with the remaining extra-virgin olive oil. Generously massage the meat with the garlic-shallot puree so that it clings to the cap of the rib roast.

3 Season the rib roast generously with the pepper and sea salt. Take the bunches of thyme and rosemary and evenly distribute them between the ribs. Tie the bunches of herbs tightly around the ends of the ribs with butcher's twine so that they will stay in place. Let the rib roast stand for 30 minutes while preparing the gas grill.

4 Preheat the gas grill to 250°F.

5 Add the hickory or maple wood chips to a small bowl filled with water and let soak. Set alongside the grill.

6 Spit the rib roast with the rotisserie's prongs so that the spit goes through the center of the rib roast toward the bone. Truss the rib roast with butcher's twine around the spit as an extra precaution.

7 Set a large aluminum roasting pan on the grill and then place the rib roast on the rotisserie above the pan, so that the juices will fall into the dish.

8 Cover the grill and roast the prime rib at a low speed for about 2 hours (16 to 18 minutes per pound, to be more exact). At this point, an instant read thermometer should record the internal heat as below 125°F.

9 Heat the smoking box and when hot, throw a handful of wood chips into the heat periodically so that you continuously smoke the prime rib while it finishes roasting—about another 30 minutes, until the thermometer reads 125°F.

10 Remove the rib roast from the rotisserie and transfer to a large carving board. Let stand for 10 minutes before carving, allowing the meat to properly store its juices.

Charcoal Pit Prime Rib

YIELD: 6 TO 8 SERVINGS • ACTIVE TIME: 1 HOUR AND 30 MINUTES • TOTAL TIME: 4 HOURS

Charcoal gives your prime rib an authentic grilling taste. It's important to note that the roasting temperature is just 325°F and the total roasting time is a little more than 2 hours.

INGREDIENTS

1 (6-rib) beef rib roast

3 tablespoons extra-virgin olive oil

2 tablespoons coarsely ground black pepper

2 tablespoons coarse sea salt

4 garlic cloves, minced

3 bunches fresh thyme

3 bunches fresh rosemary

1 Rub the rib roast with 1 tablespoon of the extra-virgin olive oil and let rest at room temperature for 30 minutes.

2 Season the rib roast generously with the pepper and sea salt.

3 In a small bowl, combine the minced garlic and the remaining extra-virgin olive oil, and then massage this marinade into the meat side of the rib roast. Take the bunches of thyme and rosemary and evenly distribute between the ribs. Tie the bunches of herbs tightly around the ribs with butcher's twine so that they will stay in place when you flip the meat on the grill. Let stand for 30 minutes while preparing the charcoal grill.

4 Prepare the charcoal grill to medium-low heat.

5 When the grill is ready, at about 325°F with the coals lightly covered with ash, place the rib roast in the middle of the grill and sear each side, including the ends, for about 2 to 3 minutes each. Next, flip the rib roast so that the bone-side is pressed against the rack, and then slowly roast for about 2 hours until the rib roast is charred and an instant thermometer reads 125°F. You'll need to restock the pit with charcoal to maintain an even roasting temperature of 325°F.

6 Remove the rib roast from the grill and transfer to a large carving board. Let stand for 10 minutes before carving, allowing the meat to properly store its juices.

TIP: KEEP A KEEN EYE ON YOUR FIRE PIT, MAKING SURE THAT YOUR COOKING TEMPERATURE REMAINS CONSISTENT AND YOUR COALS ARE GIVING OFF JUST ENOUGH SMOKE SO THAT IT WON'T OVERPOWER THE MEAT.

Slow-Cooker Prime Rib

YIELD: 4 SERVINGS • ACTIVE TIME: 1 HOUR
TOTAL TIME: 6 HOURS

The simplicity of this recipe makes it perfect for afternoons when you just don't have the time to stand around and prepare a traditional full-course meal. With the slow cooker, a low temperature cooks the meat over a longer period of time, requiring little to no effort. Even here, when we consider the dry red wine and chicken stock that the prime rib cooks in for 5 hours, it's not entirely necessary to baste the roast every 30 minutes. Instead, just make sure that everything gets into the roast and that you cook it on the low setting. Other than that, just let the slow cooker do all the work for you.

INGREDIENTS

1 (3- or 4-rib) beef rib roast

2 tablespoons coarsely ground black pepper

2 tablespoons sea salt

4 garlic cloves, minced

1 teaspoon extra-virgin olive oil

4 sprigs fresh rosemary

4 sprigs fresh thyme

1 cup dry red wine

1 cup chicken stock

1 bay leaf

1 Remove the rib roast from the refrigerator 1 hour before cooking. Using your hands, thoroughly apply the coarsely ground black pepper and sea salt to the rib roast.

2 In a small bowl, mix together the minced garlic and extra-virgin olive oil, and then apply to the roast. Let the roast stand at room temperature for about 1 hour.

3 Add rosemary, thyme, red wine, chicken stock, and bay leaf to a slow cooker. Add the rib roast, fat side up, to the slow cooker. Turn the slow cooker to low and let cook for about 5 hours until an instant-read thermometer reads 130°F for medium-rare. Note that the marinade will not completely submerge the rib roast, so baste it or flip the meat halfway through the cooking time.

4 Remove the rib roast from the slow cooker and place on a large carving board. Let rest for 15 minutes before carving.

Wood-Fired Prime Rib

YIELD: 6 TO 8 SERVINGS • ACTIVE TIME: 1 HOUR AND 30 MINUTES • TOTAL TIME: 4 HOURS

INGREDIENTS

1 (6-rib) rib roast

3 tablespoons extra-virgin olive oil

4 garlic cloves, minced

1 small shallot, finely chopped

2 tablespoons coarse sea salt

2 tablespoons coarsely ground black pepper

3 bunches fresh thyme

3 bunches fresh rosemary

While grilling a rib roast over a wood fire, you'll want to be sure that the smoke does not directly rise up to the rib roast, because that will give it too much of a smoky flavor. To combat this, you may want to set up the grill so that it features both direct and indirect heating. Simply stock your wood on one side of the fire pit and then place the rib roast towards the middle of the grilling rack. The area directly above the fire is your "direct" heating zone, and the area on the opposite side that is still hot, though does not receive the same level of flame, will be your "indirect" zone.

1 Rub the rib roast with 1 tablespoon of the extra-virgin olive oil and let rest at room temperature for 1 hour.

2 In a small bowl, combine the minced garlic and finely chopped shallot with the remaining extra-virgin olive oil. After the rib roast has rested at room temperature for about an hour, generously massage the meat with the garlic-shallot puree so that it clings to the cap of the rib roast.

3 Season the rib roast generously with the pepper and sea salt. Take the bunches of thyme and rosemary and evenly distribute between the ribs. Tie the bunches of herbs tightly around the ribs with butcher's twine so that they will stay in place when you flip the meat on the grill. Once again, let the rib roast stand for 30 minutes while preparing the charcoal grill.

4 Prepare the wood fire to feature both direct and indirect heating at an average medium-low heat of about 325°F. You'll want to make sure that you have a strong foundational layer of coals so that you can easily maintain the heat and smoke as you grill your prime rib.

5 When the fire is ready, at about 325°F with the logs lightly covered with ash, place the rib roast towards the middle of the grill (in between both heating zones, away from the smoke) and sear each side, including the ends, for about 2 to 3 minutes each. Next, flip the rib roast so that the bone-side is pressed against the rack, and then slowly roast for about 2 hours until the rib roast is charred and an instant thermometer reads 125°F.

6 Remove the rib roast from the grill and transfer to a large carving board. Let stand for 10 minutes before carving, allowing the meat to properly store its juices.

TIP: THE CHOICE OF WOOD YOU USE FOR YOUR FIRE IS ALWAYS ESSENTIAL TO THE GRILLING FLAVOR OF YOUR MEAT. FOR A MORE MEDIUM LEVEL OF FLAVOR, GO WITH A HICKORY OR OAK WOOD, GIVING YOUR RIB ROAST JUST THE RIGHT AMOUNT OF SMOKE FLAVOR. IF YOU'D LIKE MORE OF A KICK TO YOUR RIB ROAST, ADD A LOG OR TWO OF MESQUITE ONTO A FIRE THAT'S ALREADY ROOTED WITH HICKORY OR MAPLE WOOD.

Smoked Prime Rib

YIELD: 6 TO 8 SERVINGS • ACTIVE TIME: 2 HOURS
TOTAL TIME: 6 HOURS

INGREDIENTS

1 (6-rib) rib roast

3 tablespoons extra-virgin olive oil

4 garlic cloves, minced

1 small shallot, finely chopped

2 tablespoons coarse sea salt

2 tablespoons coarsely ground black pepper

3 bunches fresh thyme

3 bunches fresh rosemary

4 cups hickory or maple wood chips

The key to a properly smoked rib roast lies in the fire. As with the Wood-Fired Prime Rib (see page 82) the wood chips you chose will greatly influence the flavor of your meat. Be sure to soak your wood chips for about an hour before using on the grill, and after dispersing on top of the coals, cover the grill and align the air vent away from the fire so that the smoke will build underneath the lid and pillow over the meat. If you'd like more of a barbecued smoke flavor, mix 1 cup of mesquite wood chips with 2 cups of hickory or maple wood chips and then soak before throwing onto the flames.

1 Rub the rib roast with 1 tablespoon of the extra-virgin olive oil and let rest at room temperature for 1 hour.

2 In a small bowl, combine the minced garlic and finely chopped shallot with the 2 remaining tablespoons of extra-virgin olive oil. After the rib roast has rested at room temperature for about an hour, lowering the internal temperature of the meat so that it takes on flavors more easily, generously massage the meat with the garlic-shallot puree so that it clings to the cap of the rib roast.

3 Season the rib roast generously with the pepper and sea salt. Take the bunches of thyme and rosemary and evenly distribute between the ribs. Tie the bunches of herbs tightly around the ribs with butcher's twine so that they will stay in place when you flip the meat on the grill. Let the rib roast stand for 30 minutes while preparing the charcoal grill.

4 Prepare the fire to feature both direct and indirect heat with an average low temperature of about 300°F. You'll want to make sure that you have a strong foundational layer of coals so that you can easily maintain the heat and smoke as you grill your prime rib. While you prepare your grill, add the 4 cups of hickory or maple wood chips to a bowl of warm water and set aside.

5 When the fire is ready, at about 300°F with the coals lightly covered with ash, place the rib roast over the direct heat of the grill and sear each side, including the ends, for about 2 to 3 minutes each. Transfer the rib roast over the direct heat and flip the rib roast to meat side up. Take a handful of wood chips and throw them over the flame. Cover the grill, aligning the air vent away from the flame so that the smoke pillows around the rib roast, and begin slowly roasting for about 3 to 4 hours until the rib roast is charred and an instant thermometer reads 125°F. For the first 3 hours of the grilling process, distribute handfuls of the hickory or maple wood chips about every 30 minutes or so.

6 Remove the rib roast from the grill and transfer to a large carving board. Let stand for 10 minutes before carving, allowing the meat to properly store its juices.

One-Pot Prime Rib

Here, technique is key. This prime rib is structured on a simple recipe that will give you a full meal all in one. You'll need a large Dutch oven, or a large roasting pan will work as well. For the red wine base, try a full-body red wine. And pour a glass for yourself.

INGREDIENTS

1 (4-rib) rib roast, frenched

2 tablespoons coarsely ground black pepper

2 tablespoons sea salt

1 tablespoon, plus 1 teaspoon extra-virgin olive oil

2 bunches fresh rosemary

2 bunches fresh thyme

12 large carrots, peeled and chopped into 2-inch segments

2 large white onions, diced

8 medium russet potatoes

1 cup dry red wine

1½ cups beef broth

1 bay leaf

1 Remove the rib roast from the refrigerator 1 hour before cooking. Using your hands, thoroughly apply the coarsely ground black pepper and sea salt to the rib roast.

2 Next, in a small bowl, mix together the minced garlic and 1 teaspoon of the extra-virgin olive oil, and then apply to the roast. Break apart the rosemary and thyme bunches into quarters and then evenly distribute the sprigs between the bones on the top of the roast. Tie the herbs firmly to the roast with butcher's twine. Let the roast stand at room temperature for about 1 hour.

3 Prepare the oven to 425°F.

4 Place a small roasting rack in the Dutch oven or roasting pan (if you don't have a rack that will fit in the Dutch oven, simply line the bottom of the pot with several sheets of aluminum foil.) Next, space a sheet or two of aluminum foil evenly across the roasting rack, and then place the Dutch oven or roasting pan in the oven while it heats.

5 Place the carrots, onions, and potatoes in the bottom of the Dutch oven or roasting pan. Next, add the wine, beef broth, and bay leaf to the pan and stir thoroughly. Place the rib roast on the roasting rack and then transfer to the Dutch oven or roasting pan in the oven and cook for 15 minutes at 425°F so that the roast gets a good initial searing. Reduce the heat to 325°F and cook for another 3 to 4 hours, until the middle of the roast reads 125°F if tested with an instant-read thermometer.

6 A half hour before removing the roast from the oven, place the asparagus in a small baking dish, coat with the remaining extra-virgin olive oil, season with the pepper and sea salt, and then place in the oven and bake until browned, about 20 to 30 minutes. When finished, remove and cover with aluminum foil.

7 Remove the roast from the oven and let stand for 15 minutes before carving. Using a large slotted-spoon, remove the soft carrots, onions, and potatoes from the broth and let drain in a strainer.

Cowboy Steaks

**YIELD: 2 TO 3 SERVINGS • ACTIVE TIME: 15 MINUTES
TOTAL TIME: 1 HOUR AND 30 MINUTES**

Traditional rib eye steaks come straight from the rib roast. Because the prime rib is nearly always roasted (even when it's grilled, it undergoes the roasting technique), the meat develops a much richer flavor and a softer, tender consistency. However, when you slice the rib eye directly between the ribs, you'll receive a bone-in rib eye, or a classic cowboy steak. Grilling the rib eye scores the meat quickly over the flames of the grill, allowing the meat to have a tough, grainy texture that is unique to the rib eye altogether.

1 Rub both sides of the steaks with the extra-virgin olive oil and let rest at room temperature for about 1 hour.

2 A half hour before cooking, prepare the gas or charcoal grill to medium-high heat.

3 When the grill is ready, about 400 to 450°F with the coals lightly covered with ash, season one side of the steaks with half of the coarsely ground pepper and sea salt. Place the seasoned sides of the steaks on the grill and cook for about 6 to 7 minutes, until blood begins to rise from the tops. Season the tops of the steaks while you wait.

INGREDIENTS

2 bone-in rib eye steaks, about 1¼ to 1½ inches thick, cut from rib roast

2 tablespoons extra-virgin olive oil

Coarsely ground black pepper, to taste

Sea salt, to taste

4 When the steaks are charred, flip and cook for 4 to 5 more minutes for medium-rare and 5 to 6 more minutes for medium. The steaks should feel slightly firm if poked in the center.

5 Remove the steaks from the grill and transfer to a large cutting board. Let stand for 5 to 10 minutes, allowing the steaks to properly store their juices and flavor.

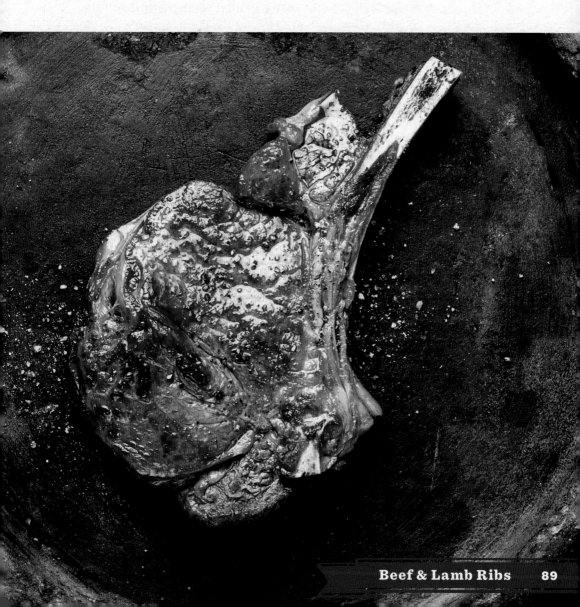

Chipotle Rib Eye

This is a spiced dish that is not for those who dislike flavor. Serve with a glass of red wine.

INGREDIENTS

For the steak

2 bone-in rib eyes, about 1¼ to 1½ inches thick

1 tablespoon olive oil

For the rub

2 dry chipotle peppers, seeded and finely minced

1 tablespoon dried oregano

1 tablespoon dried cilantro

1 tablespoon coarsely ground black pepper

2 teaspoons ground cumin

1 teaspoon onion powder

½ teaspoon dry mustard

Sea salt, to taste

1 Combine the rub ingredients and mix thoroughly.

2 Rub a very thin layer of olive oil on both sides of the steaks and then generously apply the dry rub, firmly pressing it all around the steak. Let rest at room temperature for at least 1 hour.

3 A half hour before cooking, prepare your gas or charcoal grill to medium-high heat.

4 When the grill is ready, at about 400 to 450°F with the coals lightly covered with ash, place the steaks on the grill and cook for about 6 to 7 minutes, until blood begins to rise from the tops. When the steaks are charred, flip and cook for 4 to 5 more minutes for medium-rare and 5 to 6 more minutes for medium. The steaks should feel slightly firm if poked in the center.

5 Remove the steaks from the grill and transfer to a large cutting board. Let stand for 5 to 10 minutes, allowing the steaks to properly store their juices and flavor. Serve warm.

INGREDIENTS

For the short ribs

3-4 lbs. beef short ribs, cut to 3 to 5 inches

Coarsely ground black pepper

Sea salt, to taste

For the marinade

2 cups basil leaves, finely chopped

2 large carrots, finely chopped

2 large onions, finely chopped

2 garlic cloves, finely chopped

1 scallion, finely chopped

2 sprigs fresh thyme, leaves removed

2 sprigs fresh rosemary, leaves removed

2 sprigs oregano, leaves removed

3 tablespoons olive oil

1 bottle dry red wine

Grilled Beef Short Ribs with Red Wine & Basil Marinade

YIELD: 4 TO 5 SERVINGS • ACTIVE TIME: 1 HOUR
TOTAL TIME: 8 HOURS

Beef short ribs are extremely soft and delicate after marinating. You can eat these with your hands, but set the table with forks and knives for the bits that fall off the bone.

1 The night before you plan on grilling, combine all the ingredients for the marinade, except for the wine, in a large bowl or roasting pan. Add the short ribs and pour in the wine. Move the bowl to the refrigerator and let rest for 4 to 6 hours.

2 Transfer the ribs from the marinade to a large cutting board or plate and let stand at room temperature for 1 hour. Season one side of the ribs with half of the pepper and salt.

3 A half hour before cooking, prepare your gas or charcoal grill to medium-high heat.

4 When the grill is ready, at about 400 to 450°F with the coals lightly covered with ash, place the seasoned sides of the ribs on the grill and cook for about 4 minutes. Season the tops of the ribs while waiting. When the steaks are charred, flip and cook for 4 more minutes.

5 Transfer the ribs to a cutting board and let rest for 5 to 10 minutes. Serve warm.

Beer-Marinated Prime Rib

YIELD: 6 TO 8 SERVINGS • ACTIVE TIME: 1 HOUR AND 30 MINUTES • TOTAL TIME: 6 HOURS

In the summertime, beer is the perfect marinade for any cut of red meat, though traditionally, rib roasts aren't marinated with beer too often. Since the rib roast has a dense core, the marinade will mostly penetrate the roast's cap, with a little flavor making its way to the core. Try this recipe toward the end of fall, and serve it with a porter or stout.

INGREDIENTS

1 (6-rib) rib roast

3 tablespoons coarsely ground black pepper

2 tablespoons sea salt

4 garlic cloves, minced

¼ cup, plus 2 teaspoons extra-virgin olive oil

4 sprigs fresh rosemary

4 sprigs fresh thyme

2 tablespoons soy sauce

1 teaspoon Worcestershire sauce

2 cups dark beer (brown ale, dark stout, etc.)

1 large white onion, diced

1 Place the rib roast meat side down in a large bowl or baking pan—something large enough to hold the rib roast. Next, generously season the meat with the coarsely ground black pepper and sea salt, massaging it in with your hands and making sure that the seasoning thoroughly sticks to the roast.

2 Mix the minced garlic and the 2 teaspoons of the extra-virgin olive oil in a small cup, and then brush onto the rib roast over the pepper and salt.

3 Add the remaining ingredients into the baking pan and mix thoroughly. Note that the entire rib roast will not be submerged in the marinade—part of the reason why you'll want to keep the rib roast meat side down in the baking pan—so be sure to spoon the marinade onto the rib side of the roast throughout the marinating process.

4 Transfer the baking dish into the refrigerator and let marinate for about 4 hours. Remove roast from the marinade and transfer to a large carving board 1 hour before roasting. Set the marinade aside; it will be used for basting during the roasting process.

5 Preheat the oven to 425°F.

6 Place the rib roast meat side up on a rack in the roasting pan. Lightly season again with the pepper and sea salt. When the oven is ready, transfer the rib roast to the oven and cook for 15 minutes at 450°F so that it gets a strong initial searing.

7 Reduce the heat to 325°F and continue to roast for about 3 to 4 more hours. Baste with the marinade every 30 minutes or so during the roasting process. Use the juices and marinade that accumulate at the bottom of the roasting pan as a strong base for an au jus.

8 Remove the rib roast from the oven and let stand for 15 minutes before carving, allowing it to properly store its juices and flavor.

TIP: TO MAKE THIS DISH GLUTEN-FREE, USE GLUTEN-FREE BEER AND CHECK THE LABEL ON YOUR WORCESTERSHIRE SAUCE.

Frenched Prime Rib

YIELD: 6 TO 8 SERVINGS • ACTIVE TIME: 2 HOURS
TOTAL TIME: 6 HOURS

Frenching a cut of meat isn't too challenging and is normally done when serving to impress. When you french a cut of meat, you trim the meat away from the upper portion of the bones so that when roasted, the bones flare out at the top in an elegant fashion. To french, all you need is a sharp carving knife and paring knife in order to remove the meat from the bones.

INGREDIENTS

1 (6-rib) rib roast

2 tablespoons coarse sea salt

2 tablespoons coarsely ground black pepper

¼ cup extra-virgin olive oil

6 garlic cloves, minced

1 tablespoon chopped fresh thyme, plus 3 bunches

1 tablespoon chopped fresh rosemary, plus 3 bunches

1 Remove the rib roast from the refrigerator and place on cooling racks over a large carving board, bone side down. In order to french the rib roast, you will need to cut off the meat that is on top of the bones. To do so, go about 2 inches down the ribs and using a carving knife, cut down through the meat until you reach the bone. Make a sharp cut and then cut up the bone so that the top of the meat can be peeled off. This top meat is very delicate and flavorful and works great in stews.

2 Stand the rib roast up and starting with the left bone, cut down 1 to 2 inches along the bone, cut across to the next bone, and then cut back up so that you get a rectangular chunk of the meat to come apart from the space between the ribs. Do this to all the ribs, and then gently cut away the meat so that the ribs are left to stand openly and on their own. Using a paring knife, gently scrape away any bits of meat that still cling to the ribs. Set roast aside.

3 In a small bowl, combine the 2 tablespoons of sea salt and pepper. Using your hands, massage the seasoning into the rib roast so that the grains of salt and pepper cling to it firmly.

4 In a small bowl, whisk together the extra-virgin olive oil and minced garlic, followed by the finely chopped thyme and rosemary. Brush the marinade over the rib roast, making sure that the majority of the finely chopped herbs are applied to the ends of the roast. Let the roast stand for about 30 minutes to 1 hour while you preheat the oven.

5 Preheat the oven to 450°F.

6 Using some butcher's twine, carefully tie the thyme and rosemary bunches into the spaces between the ribs so that they are firmly in place. Place the roast rib side down, meat side up on a rack in a large roasting pan. When the oven is ready, transfer the rib roast to the oven and cook for 15 minutes at 450°F so that the rib roast gets a strong initial searing. Reduce the heat to 325°F and continue to roast for about 3 to 4 more hours.

7 Toward the end of the recommended roasting time, use an instant-read thermometer to check the internal temperature of the meat. When it reads 125°F, pull the rib roast out for medium-rare.

8 Let the rib roast stand at room temperature for 10 minutes before carving, allowing it to properly store its juices and flavor.

Crowned Roast of Beef

YIELD: 12 SERVINGS • ACTIVE TIME: 2 HOURS
TOTAL TIME: 5 HOURS

Although crowning a roast of meat is traditionally done more often for roasts of pork and lamb, you can also crown a roast of beef. It's a little more challenging and requires you to do so on a larger cut of prime rib–about 10 ribs. Built upon the fundamental method of frenching the meat, a crowned prime rib has the frenched ribs at the top, though it's sliced and bent into a circle so that the ribs, when positioned properly, resemble a crown. Butcher's twine is definitely required here.

INGREDIENTS

1 (10-rib) rib roast

3 tablespoons coarsely ground black pepper

3 tablespoons sea salt

1 cup extra-virgin olive oil

8 garlic cloves, minced

1/3 cup fresh thyme, coarsely chopped

1/3 cup fresh rosemary, coarsely chopped

4 tablespoons fresh sage, finely chopped

1 Remove the rib roast from the refrigerator and place it on cooling racks over a large carving board, bone-side down. To begin, you will need to french the rib roast. First, cut the meat that covers the bones. To do so, go about 2 inches down the ribs and using a sharp carving knife, cut through the meat until you reach the bone. Make a sharp cut and then cut up the bone so that the top of the meat can be peeled off.

2 Stand the rib roast up and starting with the left bone, cut down 1 to 2 inches along the bone, across to the next bone, and then back up so that you get a rectangular chunk of the meat to come apart from the space between the ribs. Do this to all the ribs, and then gently cut away the meat so that the ribs are left to stand openly and on their own. Using a paring knife, gently scrape away any bits of meat that still cling to the ribs.

3 Bring the meat together into a circle, cut about ½ to 1 inch into the meat side of the rib roast between each bone. Make your cuts even and leveled. Stand the rib roast and, pushing back the ends of the roast, form it into a tight crown. Note that because it's fairly difficult to crown a roast of beef, you may need to cut deeper than 1 inch between the ribs so that it allows for more flexibility. Using butcher's twine, tie the crown tightly so that it'll remain in that position while roasting—you'll need to tie the roast around the bones themselves, and also around the equator of the roast. Set aside.

4 Mix the pepper and sea salt in a small bowl. Using your hands, massage the seasoning into the rib roast.

5 In a small bowl whisk together the remaining ingredients. Using your hands, massage the paste into the rib roast. Let stand at room temperature for 30 minutes to 1 hour.

6 Preheat the oven to 450°F.

7 Place the standing rib roast in a large roasting pan on a large sheet of flat roasting racks. Cover the crown with aluminum foil so that it keeps the heat central. Roast at 450°F for 15 minutes so that the rib roast receives a nice initial searing. Lower the heat to 325°F and cook for another 2 to 3 hours, until the internal temperature of the meat reads 125°F for medium-rare. Baste the rib roast with its own juices every 30 minutes or so.

8 Remove the crown roast from the oven and place on a large serving piece. Let stand for 10 minutes before carving.

Californian Coffee Prime Rib

YIELD: 6 TO 8 SERVINGS • ACTIVE TIME: 1 HOUR
TOTAL TIME: 4 HOURS

A coffee-based rub is nearly always paired with beef because of its bold, but soft flavors. The coffee rub is heavy, but it's very accessible because its flavors largely remain on the outside of the roast. When applied to the rib roast, the flavors might get into the cap of the roast, though for the most part, the finely ground coffee and split peppercorns will form a thick, charred crust on the outside of the roast.

INGREDIENTS

1 (6-rib) beef rib roast

2 tablespoons whole black peppercorns

2 tablespoons sea salt

¼ cup finely ground coffee

3 tablespoons thyme, finely chopped

2 tablespoons dark brown sugar

2 teaspoons ground mustard

1 teaspoon smoked paprika

3 tablespoons extra-virgin olive oil

3 bunches fresh rosemary (optional)

1 Remove the rib roast from the refrigerator 1 hour before cooking and let stand at room temperature.

2 Preheat the oven to 450°F.

3 Place the whole black peppercorns in a small, sealable bag and seal tightly. Place the bag on a flat surface and then, using the bottom of a heavy pan such as a cast-iron skillet, firmly pound the peppercorns so that they split into large pieces. Ideally, you'll want the peppercorns to be much more coarse than what a traditional pepper mill will do. Remove the split peppercorns from the bag and add to a small bowl. Mix in the sea salt.

4 Add the next 6 ingredients to the salt and peppercorns and combine so it forms an evenly-distributed rub.

5 Next, when the meat's temperature has lowered, generously apply the extra-virgin olive oil to the prime rib. Using your hands, apply the rub to the prime rib, making sure that all areas of the meat under the fat-cap also receive the rub. If desired, divide the bunches of rosemary evenly and place inbetween the ribs. Tie firmly with butcher's twine so the rosemary stays in place while roasting.

6 Transfer the coffee-rubbed prime rib to a large rack set in a roasting pan. Then transfer the pan to the oven and sear for about 15 minutes.

7 Reduce the heat to 325°F and cook for 2½ to 3 hours, until a thermometer registers 125°F for medium-rare. During the roasting process, the crust of the rib roast may begin to brown—if that is the case, gently cover the rib roast with a sheet of aluminum foil in order to help maintain the moisture on the cap of the roast.

8 Remove the rib roast from the oven, transfer to a large carving board, and let stand for about 10 minutes before carving, allowing it to properly store its juices and flavor.

INGREDIENTS

For the ribs

1 (3-lb.) whole beef ribs rack, trimmed

2 tablespoons kosher salt

1 tablespoon black pepper

1 cup beef stock

For the farofa

2 tablespoons unsalted butter

2 cups manioc flour

2 scallions, green tops only, sliced

1 handful fresh parsley, torn

Churrasco Ribs with Farofa

YIELD: 4 SERVINGS • ACTIVE TIME: 30 MINUTES
TOTAL TIME: 7 HOURS

In Brazil, the Portuguese word *churrasco* refers to both grilled beef and meat in general. *Farofa* is a staple side dish with grilled meat; its foundation is the coarse manioc flour, also known as cassava flour or tapioca flour, which is then seasoned with everything from scallions and olives to raisins.

1 Preheat oven or grill to 275°F.

2 To begin preparations for the ribs, rub both sides of ribs with salt and black pepper. Place on a roasting trivet set inside a large roasting pan lined with aluminum foil.

3 Roast ribs until very tender, about 6 hours, basting from time to time with beef stock. When the ribs are ready, the meat should be falling away from the bones.

4 To begin preparations for the *farofa*, melt the butter in a saucepan set over medium heat. Add the manioc flour, toasting in the butter until golden and fragrant, about 3 to 4 minutes.

5 Remove the *farofa* from heat and season to taste with salt and pepper. Cover and set aside until ready to serve.

6 When ready, remove ribs from the oven or grill. Let rest under aluminum foil for 10 minutes. Garnish the *farofa* with the scallions and parsley and serve alongside the ribs.

BBQ Lamb Ribs

YIELD: 4 SERVINGS • ACTIVE TIME: 1 HOUR
TOTAL TIME: 24 HOURS

Lamb is often thought of as being "gamy," but when cooked with this sweet sauce no one will be able to make that claim.

INGREDIENTS

2 sprigs fresh rosemary

2 cloves garlic, crushed

1 cup distilled white vinegar

¾ cup ketchup

2 teaspoons honey

1 teaspoon Worcestershire sauce

¾ cup dark brown sugar

1 tablespoon chili powder

1½ teaspoons kosher salt

1 teaspoon black pepper

2 (3-lb.) racks lamb ribs, trimmed

1 Combine all of the ingredients except for the ribs in a saucepan.

2 Bring to a boil over a high heat before reducing to a simmer; cook until thickened, about 20 to 30 minutes. Set aside to cool for 30 minutes.

3 Place ribs on a roasting trivet set inside a large roasting dish lined with aluminum foil. Brush half the sauce onto ribs. Cover with aluminum foil and refrigerate overnight.

4 The next day, preheat a gas or charcoal grill to 250°F; if using charcoal, prepare coals on one side of grill. Place ribs in oven or on grill and cook until dark brown and tender, about 3 hours; baste with remaining barbecue sauce from time to time.

5 When ready, remove ribs from heat and let rest under aluminum foil for 10 minutes.

6 Cut between bones to separate ribs before serving.

INGREDIENTS

For the ribs

2 tablespoons kosher salt

2 tablespoons brown sugar

2 tablespoon coffee grounds, freshly ground to a fine powder

1 teaspoon black pepper

1 teaspoon mustard powder

1 (4-lb.) rack lamb ribs, cleaned and trimmed

For the mop sauce

2 cups apple cider vinegar

½ teaspoon kosher salt

2 tablespoons molasses

½ teaspoon black pepper

1 pinch cayenne

1 pinch red pepper flakes

Grilled Lamb Ribs

YIELD: 4 SERVINGS • ACTIVE TIME: 45 MINUTES
TOTAL TIME: 3 HOURS AND 30 MINUTES

Coffee grounds add both a floral and flavorful note to this recipe that is sure to perk up your taste buds.

1 To begin preparations for the ribs, combine salt, sugar, coffee, black pepper, and mustard powder in a small bowl.

2 Rub seasoning mix into ribs, letting them sit at room temperature for 1 hour.

3 To prepare for the mop sauce, whisk together everything for the sauce in a bowl until the molasses dissolves.

4 Preheat a gas or charcoal grill to 325°F. Place ribs on grill and cook, turning once, until golden-brown, about 12 to 15 minutes total.

5 Reduce temperature to 250°F and grill until tender, turning and basting with mop sauce every 10 to 15 minutes, about 1 hour and 30 minutes.

6 When ribs are tender and the meat is falling away from the bones, remove and let rest under aluminum foil for 10 minutes.

7 Pour any remaining mop sauce into a saucepan and bring to a boil over high heat, cooking until slightly reduced, about 2 to 4 minutes.

8 Cut between bones to separate ribs, brushing with reduced mop sauce and serving remainder on side.

Chargrilled Lamb Ribs with Coriander & Pepper

YIELD: 4 SERVINGS • ACTIVE TIME: 30 MINUTES
TOTAL TIME: 3 HOURS

Coriander seeds are subtly aromatic, lending themselves well to the grassy quality of lamb.

INGREDIENTS

3 tablespoons coriander seeds, lightly crushed

1 tablespoon kosher salt

2 teaspoons red pepper flakes

2 teaspoons black pepper

1 pinch cayenne

1 (4-lb.) rack lamb ribs, cleaned and trimmed

1 cup apple cider vinegar

3 tablespoons brown sugar

2 tablespoons olive oil

1 Stir together the coriander, salt, red pepper flakes, black pepper, and cayenne in a small bowl. Rub about two-thirds into ribs, letting them sit at room temperature for 1 hour.

2 Whisk vinegar, sugar, and olive oil into remaining spice mix. Cover and set aside.

3 Preheat a gas or charcoal grill to 325°F. Place ribs on grill and cook, turning once, until golden-brown, about 10 minutes.

4 Reduce temperature to 250°F, or move the ribs away from the coals on a charcoal grill, and grill until tender, about 1½ hours, turning and basting with prepared sauce every 10 to 15 minutes.

5 Remove the ribs and let rest under aluminum foil for 10 minutes before cutting ribs and serving.

INGREDIENTS

2 tablespoons fennel seeds,
lightly toasted

2 tablespoons sesame seeds

1½ teaspoons red pepper
flakes

1 tablespoon flaked sea salt

2 teaspoons black
peppercorns, lightly crushed

1 (4-lb.) rack lamb ribs,
trimmed

¾ cup dark soy sauce

1 cup rice vinegar

2 teaspoons sugar

3 red Thai chilies, finely
chopped

2 scallions, greens only,
sliced, for garnish

Chili Vinegar Lamb Ribs

YIELD: 4 SERVINGS • ACTIVE TIME: 1 HOUR
TOTAL TIME: 7 HOURS

Lamb is used widely in parts of China and Mongolia, making the ingredients in this recipe a natural fit.

1 In a mixing bowl, stir together fennel seeds, sesame seeds, red pepper flakes, sea salt, and peppercorns.

2 Rub about half the spice mixture onto meat side of ribs. Set ribs on a roasting trivet set inside a large roasting dish lined with aluminum foil. Cover and refrigerate for at least 4 hours, preferably longer.

3 When ready to cook, preheat a gas or charcoal grill to 325°F. Make sure to bank coals to one side if using a charcoal grill. Place ribs on grill and cook, turning once, until golden-brown, about 10 minutes total.

4 In the meantime, stir together the soy sauce, vinegar, sugar, and chilies in a small bowl until the sugar dissolves. Divide chili vinegar between two bowls.

5 Reduce grill temperature to 250°F and continue grilling ribs until tender, turning and basting with chili vinegar from one bowl every 10 to 15 minutes. Total cooking time for the ribs is about 1 hour and 45 minutes.

6 When ready, place ribs on a platter and let rest under aluminum foil for 10 minutes. Cut between bones to separate them.

7 Sprinkle with remaining spice mix and the scallions over the ribs and serve with the reserved bowl of chili vinegar.

Spicy Lamb Ribs with Tzatziki & Lemon

YIELD: 4 SERVINGS • ACTIVE TIME: 30 MINUTES
TOTAL TIME: 3 HOURS

Lamb ribs can be hard to source; check with your local butcher for the best results.

1 Stir together the salt, sugar, cumin, coriander, and black pepper in a small bowl. Rub half into ribs, letting them sit at room temperature for 1 hour.

2 Whisk vinegar into the remaining spice mix. Cover and set aside.

3 Preheat a gas or charcoal grill to 325°F. Make sure to bank the coals to one side if using a charcoal grill. Place ribs on the grill and cook, turning once, until browned, about 10 minutes.

4 Reduce temperature to 250°F, or move ribs away from the coals on a charcoal grill, and grill until tender, about 1½ hours, turning and basting with prepared sauce every 10 to 15 minutes.

5 Remove the ribs and let rest under aluminum foil for 10 minutes. Cut into individual ribs. Place the tzatziki in a bowl, drizzle with olive oil, and sprinkle the parsley on top. Serve alongside the ribs and lemon wedges.

INGREDIENTS

2 tablespoons kosher salt

2 tablespoons brown sugar

1 tablespoon freshly
ground cumin

1 tablespoon freshly
ground coriander

½ teaspoon black pepper

1 (4-lb.) rack lamb ribs,
cleaned and trimmed

²⁄₃ cup apple cider vinegar

Tzatziki, for serving

Olive oil, for serving

1 handful fresh parsley,
for serving

Lemon wedges, for serving

INGREDIENTS

For the ribs

1 tablespoon kosher salt

1 tablespoon sugar

1 teaspoon black pepper

1 teaspoon Chinese five-spice powder

1 (4-lb.) rack lamb ribs, trimmed

For the Yakiniku sauce

1 garlic clove, chopped

½ cup yuzu juice

⅓ cup soy sauce

3 tablespoons mirin

3 tablespoons sugar

2 teaspoons honey

2 teaspoons sesame oil

1 tablespoon cornstarch, mixed to a slurry with 1 tablespoon water

2 teaspoons sesame seeds, toasted and ground

Yuzu Sesame Lamb Ribs

YIELD: 4 SERVINGS • ACTIVE TIME: 1 HOUR
TOTAL TIME: 4 HOURS

Yuzu is a fragrant and tart citrus fruit that is the base of this Japanese-style *yakiniku* sauce.

1 To begin preparations for the ribs, stir together salt, sugar, black pepper, and five-spice powder in a small bowl. Rub mixture into ribs, letting them sit at room temperature for 1 hour.

2 To begin preparations for the sauce, combine everything for the sauce, except the cornstarch slurry and the ground sesame seeds, in a saucepan. Bring to a boil over medium heat and then reduce to a simmer until slightly thickened, about 5 minutes.

3 Strain sauce into a small saucepan and return to a simmer. Whisk in cornstarch slurry and ground sesame seeds, returning to a simmer until sauce has thickened. Remove from heat and cover until ready to use.

4 Preheat a gas or charcoal grill to 325°F. Make sure to bank coals to one side if using a charcoal grill. Place the ribs on the grill and cook, turning once, until browned, about 10 minutes total.

5 Reduce temperature to 250°F, or move the ribs away from the coals on a charcoal grill, and cook until tender, about 1 hour and 45 minutes, turning and basting with prepared sauce every 10 to 15 minutes.

6 Remove ribs and let rest under aluminum foil for 10 minutes. Cut rack into double ribs to serve.

Grill-Roasted Rack of Lamb with Garlic-Herb Crust

YIELD: 5 TO 6 SERVINGS • ACTIVE TIME: 20 MINUTES
TOTAL TIME: 14 HOURS

Because the rack of lamb is a very delicate meat, be sure to give it the time to marinate overnight. Pair this with a glass of red wine.

1 The night before grilling, combine the olive oil, garlic, and lemon zest in a large sealable plastic bag. Pat dry the racks of lamb, then season them with coarsely ground black pepper and sea salt, kneading the pepper and salt deeply into the meaty sections of the lamb. Place the racks of lamb into a plastic bag and place in the refrigerator. Let marinate overnight.

2 An hour and a half before grilling, remove the racks of lamb from the refrigerator and let rest, uncovered and at room temperature.

3 A half hour before grilling, prepare your gas or charcoal grill to medium heat.

4 While the grill heats, combine all of the ingredients for the garlic-herb crust in a small bowl. Next, take the racks of lamb and generously apply the crust ingredients to it, being sure to apply the majority of the crust on the meaty side of the rack.

5 When the grill is ready, at about 400°F with the coals lightly covered with ash, place the meat-side of the racks of lamb on the grill and cook for about 3 to 4 minutes. When the crusts are browned, flip the racks of lamb and grill for another 5 minutes for medium-rare.

6 Transfer the racks of lamb from the grill to a large carving board and let rest for about 10 minutes before slicing between the ribs. Serve warm.

INGREDIENTS

For the ribs

2 tablespoons olive oil

2 garlic cloves, finely chopped

1 teaspoon lemon zest

2 (8-rib) racks of lamb, about 1 lb. each

Coarsely ground black pepper, to taste

Sea salt, to taste

For the garlic-herb crust

4 garlic cloves, finely chopped

½ small shallot, finely chopped

¼ cup flat-leaf parsley, coarsely chopped

2 tablespoons rosemary, finely chopped

1 tablespoon thyme, finely chopped

1 tablespoon olive oil

Coarsely ground black pepper, to taste

Sea salt, to taste

Beef & Lamb Ribs

Lamb Chops with Paprika-Salt Rub

YIELD: 4 SERVINGS • ACTIVE TIME: 15 MINUTES
TOTAL TIME: 1 HOUR AND 30 MINUTES

The paprika-salt is a spice both soft and strong at the same time.

1 An hour before grilling, brush the meat on the lamb rib chops with olive oil and let stand at room temperature.

2 In a small bowl, mix together the remaining ingredients to make the paprika-salt rub. Using your hands, generously apply the rub to the lamb rib chops.

3 Prepare your gas or charcoal grill to medium-high heat.

4 When the grill is ready, at about 400 to 450°F with the coals lightly covered with ash, place the lamb rib chops on the grill and cook for about 4 minutes, or until the spices have browned. Turn the chops and cook for another 3 to 4 minutes for medium-rare, and 4 to 5 minutes for medium.

5 Transfer the lamb rib chops to a large carving board and let stand for 5 minutes before serving.

INGREDIENTS

12 lamb rib chops, each about 1 inch thick

2 tablespoons olive oil

2 tablespoons smoked paprika

1 tablespoon cumin seeds

2 teaspoons coriander seeds

½ teaspoon cayenne pepper

Coarsely ground black pepper, to taste

Sea salt, to taste

Marinades, Rubs & Sauces

The following is a selection of flavorful marinades, rubs, and sauces that work for any type of ribs. From the bright bursts of Citrus Marinade (see page 125), to the punch of a Hot & Spicy Chili Rub (see page 168), the sweetness of Bourbon & Sugar Glaze (see page 145), and the rich, smoky flavor of 12 Bones Blueberry-Chipotle Barbecue Sauce (see page 158) from 12 Bones Smokehouse in Asheville, North Carolina, there is a recipe for everyone. Feel free to experiment with flavor profiles to find what best suits your tastes in your pursuit for the perfect ribs.

Balsamic Marinade

YIELD: ABOUT 2 CUPS • ACTIVE TIME: 10 MINUTES
TOTAL TIME: 4 TO 24 HOURS

INGREDIENTS

4 sprigs fresh basil

2 sprigs fresh rosemary, leaves removed

2 garlic cloves, crushed

2 teaspoons Dijon mustard

1 teaspoon raw honey

1 cup olive oil

¼ cup balsamic vinegar

1 tablespoon black pepper

1 tablespoon sea salt

1 In a medium bowl or roasting pan, combine all the marinade ingredients and let rest for 15 minutes in order for the flavors to spread throughout the marinade.

2 Add your desired meat into the marinade. Transfer to the refrigerator and let marinate from 4 hours to overnight. The marinade may not fully cover the meat. In that case, turn the meat halfway through the marinating process so that all areas of the meat receive equal amounts of the marinade.

Marinades, Rub & Sauces

Citrus Marinade

YIELD: ABOUT 2 CUPS • ACTIVE TIME: 15 MINUTES
TOTAL TIME: 2 HOURS AND 15 MINUTES

1 Put all the marinade ingredients in a bowl large enough to also accommodate the meat. If the meat isn't fully submerged in the marinade, rotate it a couple of times.

2 Add the meat into the marinade and let marinate for 2 hours in the refrigerator. The meat will not be fully submerged in the marinade, so be sure to rotate it throughout the marinating process in order for all sides of the roast to receive equal marinating time.

3 A half hour before roasting, remove the meat from the marinade and place on the roasting rack so that the marinade seeps from the meat. Discard the remaining marinade.

INGREDIENTS

¾ cup orange juice

½ medium lime, juiced

½ medium lemon, juiced

¼ cup cilantro, finely chopped

¼ cup extra-virgin olive oil

2 tablespoons rosemary, finely chopped

4 garlic cloves, minced

1 tablespoon black pepper

1 tablespoon sea salt

Five-Spice Marinade

YIELD: 1½ CUPS • ACTIVE TIME: 10 MINUTES
TOTAL TIME: ABOUT 4 HOURS

INGREDIENTS

¾ cup soy sauce

¼ cup vinegar

2 tablespoons fresh ginger, minced

2 teaspoons sesame oil

2 teaspoons five-spice powder

¼ cup olive oil

1 teaspoon black pepper

1 In a bowl, combine all of the ingredients until they are well mixed.

2 Apply marinade to meat immediately and marinate for at least 4 hours.

Apple Cider Marinade

YIELD: ABOUT 2½ CUPS • **ACTIVE TIME: 10 MINUTES**
TOTAL TIME: 4 TO 24 HOURS

1 In a medium bowl or roasting pan, combine all the ingredients to the marinade and let rest for 15 minutes for the flavors to spread throughout the marinade.

2 Add your desired meat into the marinade. Transfer to the refrigerator and let marinate from 4 hours to overnight. If the marinade does not fully cover the meat, turn the meat halfway through the marinating process so that all areas of the meat receive equal amounts of the marinade.

INGREDIENTS

2 cups fresh apple cider

¼ cup olive oil

½ lemon, juiced

2 sprigs fresh thyme, leaves removed and finely chopped

2 sprigs fresh rosemary, leaves removed and finely chopped

2 garlic cloves, minced

1 tablespoon black pepper

2 teaspoons sea salt

Jamaican Jerk Marinade

**YIELD: ABOUT ¾ CUP • ACTIVE TIME: 10 MINUTES
TOTAL TIME: 10 MINUTES**

INGREDIENTS

1 medium onion, finely chopped

¼ cup scallions, finely chopped

1 scotch bonnet pepper, chopped

3 tablespoons soy sauce

1 tablespoon white vinegar

3 tablespoons olive oil

2 teaspoons thyme leaves, chopped

2 teaspoons sugar

1 teaspoon sea salt

1 teaspoon black pepper

1 teaspoon allspice

½ teaspoon nutmeg

½ teaspoon cinnamon

1 Place all of the ingredients into a blender and pulse to the desired consistency. Remove and marinate meat immediately.

TIP: FOR A SMOKIER FLAVOR, CONSIDER ADDING 1 OR 2 TEASPOONS OF LIQUID SMOKE (LIKE COLGIN'S) TO THE INGREDIENTS.

Marinades, Rub & Sauces

Pineapple Marinade

**YIELD: 2 CUPS • ACTIVE TIME: 10 MINUTES
TOTAL TIME: 30 MINUTES**

---

1 In a bowl, combine all of the ingredients until the sugar has dissolved completely.

2 Place meat in the marinade and marinate for at least 30 minutes.

INGREDIENTS

1½ cups pineapple juice

¼ cup brown sugar

¼ cup soy sauce

2 garlic cloves, minced

1 teaspoon sea salt

Red Wine & Dijon Marinade

YIELD: ABOUT 1 CUP • ACTIVE TIME: 20 MINUTES
TOTAL TIME: 3½ HOURS

INGREDIENTS

¾ cup dry red wine

¼ cup extra-virgin olive oil

2 garlic cloves, minced

1 tablespoon Dijon mustard

1 tablespoon black pepper

1 tablespoon sea salt

1 teaspoon rosemary, finely chopped

1 Add all of the ingredients to a large bowl that will be able to hold the meat. Transfer the marinade into the refrigerator and let stand for about 45 minutes.

2 Add the meat into the marinade and let marinate for 2 hours in the refrigerator. If the meat isn't fully submerged in the marinade, rotate it a couple of times.

3 A half hour before roasting, remove the meat from the marinade and place on the roasting rack so that the marinade seeps from the meat.

4 While cooking, baste the rib roast with the remaining marinade about every half hour.

Sweet Teriyaki Marinade

YIELD: ABOUT 1 CUP • ACTIVE TIME: 10 MINUTES
TOTAL TIME: 4 HOURS

1 In a bowl, combine all of the ingredients until the sugar has dissolved completely.

2 Apply marinade to meat immediately and marinate in the refrigerator for at least 4 hours.

INGREDIENTS

½ cup soy sauce

¼ cup brown sugar

2 tablespoons rice vinegar

2 garlic cloves, minced

2 teaspoons ginger, minced

1 teaspoon black pepper

Tandoori Marinade

YIELD: 2¼ CUPS • ACTIVE TIME: 10 MINUTES
TOTAL TIME: ABOUT 3 HOURS

INGREDIENTS

2 tablespoons olive oil

2 garlic cloves, minced

½ teaspoon ground turmeric

2 tablespoons cumin powder

1 tablespoon fresh ginger, minced

1 teaspoon paprika

1 teaspoon coriander seeds

3 tablespoons cilantro, minced

½ small lime, juiced

1½ cups plain yogurt

1 In a small skillet, heat the olive oil over medium heat. Add the remaining ingredients, except for the lime juice and yogurt, to the skillet and toast for 2 minutes. The spices, with the olive oil, should form a paste. If not, add more olive oil to the mixture.

2 Transfer the toasted spices to a bowl and stir in the lime juice and yogurt. Place your meat in the marinade for at least 3 hours before grilling.

Marinades, Rub & Sauces

Olive Oil & Garlic Marinade

YIELD: 2½ CUPS • ACTIVE TIME: 10 MINUTES
TOTAL TIME: 3 HOURS AND 30 MINUTES

1 Add all the ingredients of the marinade into a large bowl, large enough to hold the meat comfortably. Transfer the marinade into the refrigerator and let stand for about 45 minutes.

2 Add the meat into the marinade and let marinate for 2 hours in the refrigerator. If the meat isn't fully submerged in the marinade, rotate it a couple of times.

3 A half hour before roasting, remove the meat from the marinade and place on the roasting rack so that the marinade seeps from the meat.

INGREDIENTS

12 garlic cloves, crushed

6 sprigs rosemary, leaves removed

4 sprigs thyme, leaves removed

2½ cups extra-virgin olive oil

1 tablespoon coarsely ground black pepper

1 tablespoon sea salt

Apple Glaze

YIELD: 6 SERVINGS • ACTIVE TIME: 20 MINUTES
TOTAL TIME: 40 MINUTES

INGREDIENTS

2 tablespoons olive oil

2 garlic cloves, minced

2 cups apple cider

1 teaspoon Dijon mustard

1 teaspoon rosemary, minced

1 teaspoon black pepper

2 teaspoons sea salt

1 Heat olive oil in a saucepan over medium heat. Add garlic, and cook until golden, about 2 minutes.

2 Add the apple cider, Dijon mustard, rosemary, black pepper, and sea salt to the saucepan. Cook until the sauce has reduced by half, about 6 to 8 minutes. Season to taste with additional pepper and salt.

3 Remove from heat, let rest for 10 minutes, and then apply to meat.

Bourbon & Sugar Glaze

1 Place a saucepan over medium heat. Add butter and cook until melted.

2 Next, add bourbon, brown sugar, apple cider vinegar, and Dijon mustard to the saucepan. Add the salt and pepper. Bring to a simmer, cover the pan, and cook until the mixture has reduced by one-third, about 6 minutes.

3 Remove from heat and let settle to room temperature. Apply to meat before and during the cooking process.

INGREDIENTS

4 tablespoons unsalted butter

½ cup bourbon

½ cup brown sugar

¼ cup apple cider vinegar

1 teaspoon Dijon mustard

1 teaspoon black pepper

1 teaspoon sea salt

Sticky BBQ Glaze

YIELD: 6 SERVINGS • ACTIVE TIME: 5 MINUTES
TOTAL TIME: 5 MINUTES

INGREDIENTS

1½ cups light brown sugar

3 tablespoons apple cider
vinegar

3 tablespoons water

1 teaspoon red chili flakes

1 teaspoon Dijon mustard

1 teaspoon black pepper

1 teaspoon sea salt

1 Place all ingredients into a bowl and, using a fork, whisk until thoroughly combined.

Sweet Maple BBQ Glaze

YIELD: 6 SERVINGS • ACTIVE TIME: 15 MINUTES
TOTAL TIME: 1 HOUR

INGREDIENTS

1 tablespoon olive oil

2 garlic cloves, minced

¾ cup ketchup

1 cup apple cider

¼ cup maple syrup

2 tablespoons apple cider vinegar

1 teaspoon paprika

1 teaspoon Worcestershire sauce

1 teaspoon black pepper

1 teaspoon sea salt

1 Heat the olive oil in a saucepan over medium heat. Add the minced garlic cloves, and cook until golden, about 2 minutes.

2 Add the ketchup, apple cider, maple syrup, apple cider vinegar, paprika, and Worcestershire sauce to the saucepan. Bring to a simmer and let cook for about 10 to 15 minutes, until the sauce has reduced by half. Season to taste with ground pepper and sea salt.

3 Remove the glaze from the saucepan and let it settle to room temperature. Apply to meat before and during the cooking process.

Maple & Bourbon Barbecue Sauce

YIELD: 3 CUPS • ACTIVE TIME: 30 MINUTES
TOTAL TIME: 30 MINUTES

1 Combine all of the ingredients in a pot over medium-low heat and whisk them together.

2 Simmer for 20 minutes, until the sugar has melted and combined with the other ingredients, while stirring periodically. Do not overheat the sauce, as it will cause most of the alcohol to evaporate.

INGREDIENTS

6 oz. tomato sauce

½ cup apple cider vinegar

½ cup maple syrup

¼ cup Worcestershire sauce

1 cup bourbon

½ cup packed brown sugar

1 tablespoon liquid smoke

2 teaspoons cayenne pepper

2 teaspoons sweet paprika

2 teaspoons garlic powder

2 teaspoons onion powder

1 teaspoon cumin

1 teaspoon mustard powder

Korean BBQ Sauce

YIELD: 3 CUPS • ACTIVE TIME: 15 MINUTES
TOTAL TIME: 35 MINUTES

INGREDIENTS

½ cup soy sauce

¼ cup ketchup

¼ cup rice wine vinegar

3 tablespoons light brown sugar

1 teaspoon gochujang (red chili paste)

2 garlic cloves, minced

1 teaspoon sesame oil

1 teaspoon fresh ginger, grated

4 scallions, chopped

1 teaspoon black pepper

1 Place a small saucepan over medium heat.

2 Add the soy sauce, ketchup, rice wine vinegar, light brown sugar, gochujang, and minced garlic into the saucepan, and stir until thoroughly combined. Bring to a simmer, cover the saucepan, and let simmer for 15 to 20 minutes, until the sauce has reduced by half.

3 Stir in the remaining ingredients, cook for 2 more minutes, and remove from heat.

4 Let the sauce stand for 10 minutes before serving.

Madeira Sauce

**YIELD: 6 SERVINGS • ACTIVE TIME: 20 MINUTES
TOTAL TIME: 25 MINUTES**

1 Add the butter to a medium cast-iron skillet and warm over medium heat. Add the chopped shallot and sauté until translucent, about 4 minutes.

2 Add the flour to the pan and cook for 1 minute. Once incorporated, turn the heat to medium-low and add the dry red wine, Madeira, beef stock or broth, thyme, and rosemary.

3 Cook until the sauce has been significantly reduced, to your desired consistency, about 15 to 20 minutes.

4 When the sauce is reduced, remove the skillet from the stovetop and season with salt and pepper. Spoon the Madeira sauce over your meat of choice.

INGREDIENTS

2 tablespoons unsalted butter

1 small shallot, finely chopped

1 tablespoon all-purpose flour

¼ cup dry red wine

¾ cup Madeira

1 cup beef stock or broth

2 sprigs fresh thyme, leaves removed

2 sprigs fresh rosemary, leaves removed

Black pepper, to taste

Sea salt, to taste

TIP: IF YOU WANT A STRONGER MADEIRA SAUCE, ADD 1 TABLESPOON OF BEEF DEMI-GLACE TO THE SAUCE ALONG WITH THE BEEF STOCK. YOU CAN FIND BEEF DEMI-GLACE AT THE GROCERY STORE NEAR THE BEEF BROTHS AND STOCKS.

Maple BBQ Sauce

YIELD: 6 TO 8 SERVINGS • **ACTIVE TIME: 10 MINUTES**
TOTAL TIME: 25 MINUTES

INGREDIENTS

¼ small white onion, finely chopped

2 garlic cloves, minced

1 cup ketchup

3 tablespoons apple cider vinegar

1 tablespoon clarified unsalted butter

½ cup organic maple syrup

2 tablespoons organic molasses

2 teaspoons ground mustard

Black pepper, to taste

Sea salt, to taste

1 Place a medium saucepan over medium-high heat. When hot, add in the onion and garlic and cook until the onion is translucent and the garlic is golden, not brown—about 1 to 2 minutes.

2 Add in the remaining ingredients and bring to a boil.

3 Reduce the sauce to a simmer and then cook, uncovered, for about 20 minutes.

4 When the sauce has reduced to about 1 to 2 cups, remove from heat and refrigerate for an hour before serving.

Smoked Southern BBQ Sauce

**YIELD: 6 TO 8 SERVINGS • ACTIVE TIME: 35 MINUTES
TOTAL TIME: 55 MINUTES**

INGREDIENTS

2 to 3 cups hickory or oak wood chips

2 garlic cloves, finely chopped

1 medium white onion, finely chopped

1½ cups canned crushed tomatoes

½ cup tomato paste

¼ cup white wine vinegar

¼ cup balsamic vinegar

2 tablespoons Dijon mustard

1 medium lime, juiced

2 tablespoons ginger, finely chopped

1 teaspoon smoked paprika

½ teaspoon ground cinnamon

2 dried chipotle peppers, finely chopped

1 habanero pepper, seeded and finely chopped (optional)

1 cup water

Black pepper, to taste

Sea salt, to taste

TIP: OMIT THE HABANERO PEPPER IF YOU DON'T LIKE YOUR BARBECUE SAUCE AS HOT.

1 An hour before grilling, add the wood chips into a bowl of water and let soak.

2 Prepare your gas or charcoal grill to medium-high heat.

3 While waiting for the grill to heat up, place a small frying pan over medium heat and, when hot, add the garlic and onion and cook until the garlic has browned and the onion is translucent. Remove and set aside.

4 Transfer the cooked garlic and onion into a food processor, then add the tomatoes and tomato paste. Puree into a thick paste, and then add the remaining ingredients to the food processor and blend thoroughly. Transfer the sauce into a medium saucepan and set it near the grill.

5 When the grill is ready, about 400 to 450°F with the coals lightly covered with ash, drain 1 cup of the wood chips and spread over the coals or pour in the smoker box. Place the medium saucepan on the grill and then bring the sauce to a boil with the grill's lid covered, aligning the air vent away from the wood chips so that their smoke rolls around the sauce before escaping. Let the sauce cook for about 30 to 45 minutes, every 20 minutes adding another cup of drained wood chips, until it has reduced to about 2 cups.

6 Remove the sauce from heat and serve warm. The sauce can be kept refrigerated for up to 2 weeks.

12 Bones Blueberry-Chipotle Barbecue Sauce

YIELD: 5 CUPS • ACTIVE TIME: 30 MINUTES
TOTAL TIME: 1 HOUR

INGREDIENTS

1 pound fresh or frozen blueberries

5 oz. chipotle peppers in adobo sauce

¾ cup honey

3 cups 12 Bones Tomato "Q" Sauce (see recipe)

1 teaspoon ground ginger powder

1 In a food processor or a blender, puree the berries and the chipotles.

2 Transfer the berries and peppers to a saucepan, and add the remaining ingredients. Simmer this mixture over low heat for 30 minutes, stirring occasionally.

3 Remove the sauce from the heat and cool. The finished and cooled sauce can be stored in an airtight container in the refrigerator for up to a month.

12 Bones Tomato "Q" Sauce

**YIELD: 4 CUPS • ACTIVE TIME: 15 MINUTES
TOTAL TIME: 35 MINUTES**

1 Combine all ingredients in a medium-sized saucepan and simmer on low heat until all of the dry ingredients have dissolved, stirring occasionally with a whisk. Note that mustard powder can be a bit hard to dissolve.

INGREDIENTS

3 cups ketchup

²/₃ cup cider vinegar

½ cup blackstrap molasses

6 tablespoons Worcestershire sauce

6 tablespoons dark brown sugar

1 teaspoon granulated garlic

1 teaspoon granulated onion

1 teaspoon dry English mustard

1 teaspoon black pepper

1 teaspoon kosher salt

Coffee Rub

YIELD: 1 CUP • ACTIVE TIME: 5 MINUTES
TOTAL TIME: 5 MINUTES

INGREDIENTS

¼ cup ground coffee

2 tablespoons dark brown sugar

2 tablespoons cayenne pepper

2 tablespoons garlic powder

2 tablespoons paprika

2 tablespoons onion powder

1 tablespoon ground cumin

1 tablespoon kosher salt

1 Using a spoon, combine all of the ingredients in a small bowl and mix thoroughly. Apply to meat when finished.

Ancho Chile Rub

YIELD: 1 CUP • ACTIVE TIME: 5 MINUTES
TOTAL TIME: 5 MINUTES

1 In a small bowl, mix together all the ingredients and store at room temperature for up to 1 month.

INGREDIENTS

2 tablespoons sweet paprika

1 tablespoon ancho chile powder

1 tablespoon ground coriander

1 tablespoon ground cumin

2 teaspoons dried oregano

1 teaspoon ground allspice

1 teaspoon onion powder

½ teaspoon cinnamon

Chinese Five-Spice Rub

YIELD: ½ CUP • ACTIVE TIME: 5 MINUTES
TOTAL TIME: 5 MINUTES

---

1 Using a spoon, combine all of the ingredients in a small bowl and mix thoroughly. Apply to meat when finished.

> **TIP:** FOR MORE OF A KICK, TRY ADDING HALF OF A FINELY CHOPPED HABANERO PEPPER. BE CAREFUL, THOUGH, THE MORE SEEDS YOU INCLUDE, THE HOTTER IT WILL BECOME!

INGREDIENTS

1 tablespoon ground star anise

1 tablespoon ground cinnamon

1 tablespoon ground Sichuan peppercorn

1 tablespoon ground fennel seeds

1 tablespoon ground cloves

1 tablespoon garlic powder

1 tablespoon ground ginger

1 tablespoon sea salt

Cajun Rub

YIELD: ABOUT ¾ CUP • ACTIVE TIME: 5 MINUTES
TOTAL TIME: 5 MINUTES

INGREDIENTS

¼ cup sea salt

2 tablespoons black pepper

2 teaspoons paprika

2 teaspoons garlic powder

1 teaspoon onion powder

1 teaspoon cayenne pepper

1 teaspoon dried thyme

1 Using a spoon, combine all of the ingredients in a small bowl and mix thoroughly. Apply to meat when finished.

TIP: FOR A SMOKIER FLAVOR, CONSIDER ADDING 1 OR 2 TEASPOONS OF LIQUID SMOKE (LIKE COLGIN'S) TO THE INGREDIENTS.

Smoked Paprika Rub

YIELD: ½ CUP • ACTIVE TIME: 5 MINUTES
TOTAL TIME: 5 MINUTES

1 In a small bowl, thoroughly combine all the ingredients and store at room temperature for up to 1 month.

INGREDIENTS

2 tablespoons smoked paprika

2 teaspoons ground coriander

2 teaspoons ground cumin

1 teaspoon cayenne pepper

1 tablespoon black pepper

1 tablespoon sea salt

Hot & Spicy Chili Rub

YIELD: ABOUT ½ CUP • ACTIVE TIME: 5 MINUTES
TOTAL TIME: 5 MINUTES

INGREDIENTS

3 tablespoons chili powder

3 tablespoons smoked paprika

1 tablespoon dried oregano

2 teaspoons ground cumin

2 teaspoons black pepper

2 teaspoons sea salt

1 teaspoon dried thyme

1 In a small bowl, thoroughly combine all the ingredients for the rub and store in an airtight container at room temperature for up to 1 month.

Oregano-Garlic Rub

YIELD: ABOUT ¼ CUP • ACTIVE TIME: 5 MINUTES
TOTAL TIME: 5 MINUTES

1 In a small bowl, thoroughly combine all the ingredients for the rub and store in an airtight container at room temperature for up to 1 week.

> **TIP:** FRESH IS BEST. THE FLAVOR OF THE FRESH OREGANO LESSENS AS IT IS STORED FOR LONGER PERIODS OF TIME.

INGREDIENTS

1 tablespoon fresh oregano, finely chopped

2 garlic cloves, minced

2 sprigs fresh thyme, leaves removed

2 teaspoons black pepper

1 teaspoon sea salt

1 teaspoon ground cumin

1 teaspoon ground coriander

Southwestern Dry Rub

YIELD: ABOUT 3 TABLESPOONS • ACTIVE TIME: 5 MINUTES
TOTAL TIME: 5 MINUTES

INGREDIENTS

2 teaspoons chili powder

2 teaspoons paprika

1 teaspoon cayenne

1 teaspoon cumin

1 teaspoon ground coriander

1 teaspoon garlic, finely chopped

1 teaspoon kosher salt

1 teaspoon black pepper

1 Using a spoon, combine all of the ingredients in a small bowl and mix thoroughly. Apply to meat when finished.

TIPS: FOR MORE HEAT, ADD 1 TEASPOON OF FINELY CHOPPED HABANERO PEPPER. FOR A SMOKIER FLAVOR, CONSIDER ADDING 1 OR 2 TEASPOONS OF LIQUID SMOKE (LIKE COLGIN'S) TO THE INGREDIENTS.

St. Louis Rub

YIELD: ABOUT 1 CUP • ACTIVE TIME: 5 MINUTES
TOTAL TIME: 5 MINUTES

Using a spoon, combine all of the ingredients in a small bowl and mix thoroughly. Apply to meat when finished.

TIP: FOR A SMOKIER FLAVOR, CONSIDER ADDING 1 OR 2 TEASPOONS OF LIQUID SMOKE (LIKE COLGIN'S) TO THE INGREDIENTS.

INGREDIENTS

¼ cup paprika

3 tablespoons garlic powder

2 tablespoons black pepper

2 tablespoons kosher salt

2 tablespoons onion powder

1 tablespoon dark brown sugar

1 tablespoon ginger powder

1 tablespoon mustard powder

1 teaspoon celery salt

Snacks & Sides

Ribs complete any meal, but they taste even better when complemented with side dishes. Accompany the charred goodness of beef, pork, or lamb with these delicious snacks and sides.

Really Radish Dip

YIELD: 2 CUPS • ACTIVE TIME: 10 MINUTES
TOTAL TIME: 10 MINUTES

Though this is a simple dip to make using basic ingredients, the combination somehow tastes like a refined shrimp dip. While you might know it's a radish dip, go ahead and tell your guests it is shrimp dip, and see if the power of suggestion can turn a simple radish into a succulent shrimp.

INGREDIENTS

2 cups radishes

½ cup cream cheese, at room temperature

⅓ cup sour cream

2 tablespoons chopped chives

Salt and pepper, to taste

Hot sauce, to taste

Crudité, for serving (optional)

Crackers, for serving (optional)

1 Roughly chop the radishes to the desired chunkiness of the dip and set aside.

2 Place the cream cheese and sour cream in a bowl and stir until smooth.

3 Fold in the chives and radishes and season with salt, pepper, and hot sauce.

4 Serve with raw vegetables or crackers.

INGREDIENTS

3 lbs. green tomatoes, diced

1 large onion, diced

2 tablespoons minced ginger

2 garlic cloves, chopped

1 teaspoon mustard seeds

1 teaspoon cumin

1 teaspoon ground coriander

2 teaspoons kosher salt

½ cup honey or maple syrup

1 cup apple cider vinegar

1 cup raisins

Green Tomato Chutney

YIELD: 4 TO 6 PINTS • ACTIVE TIME: 35 MINUTES
TOTAL TIME: 5 TO 7 HOURS

Green tomato chutney was likely invented to use up the last of the tomatoes before the first frost. But you can use it all winter on pork and lamb chops, and it is also very nice as a condiment for a grilled cheese sandwich with sharp cheddar.

1 Bring water to a boil in a canning pot.

2 Place all of the ingredients in a large saucepan and bring to a boil. Reduce to a simmer and cook, stirring occasionally, until the onions and tomatoes are tender and the juices have thickened, 20 to 30 minutes.

3 Transfer the sauce to sterilized mason jars. Place the lids on the jars and secure the bands tightly. Place the jars in the boiling water for 40 minutes.

4 Use the tongs to remove the jars from the boiling water and let them cool. As they are cooling, you should hear the classic "ping and pop" sound of the lids creating a seal.

5 After 4 to 6 hours, check the lids. There should be no give in them, and they should be suctioned onto the jars. Discard any lids and food that did not seal properly.

Eggplant Dip

**YIELD: 4 SERVINGS • ACTIVE TIME: 20 MINUTES
TOTAL TIME: 1 HOUR AND 30 MINUTES**

This is a straightforward eggplant dip, much like baba ganoush but without the tahini. It is somewhat mild and is therefore a great opportunity to top with interesting spice blends. This recipe uses dukkah, an Egyptian seasoning made from coriander, cumin, sesame, and nuts; it will add a bit of crunch and plenty of flavor.

INGREDIENTS

1 large Italian eggplant, halved lengthwise

1 tablespoon olive oil, plus more as needed

1 onion, diced

2 garlic cloves, chopped

1 tablespoon maple syrup

Fresh lemon juice, to taste

Salt and pepper, to taste

2 tablespoons chopped tomato (optional)

1 tablespoon chopped fresh parsley or cilantro

1 tablespoon dukkah

Pita chips, for serving

1 Preheat oven to 350°F. Place the eggplant, cut-side down, on a greased baking sheet. Roast in the oven until the eggplant is very soft, about 30 minutes. Remove from the oven and let cool.

2 Place the oil and onion in a skillet and cook over medium heat until the onion is just beginning to brown, about 5 minutes. Add the garlic and cook 2 minutes more.

3 Remove the skin from the cooled eggplant and add the flesh to the pan. Cook the eggplant until it breaks down further and becomes extremely tender, about 5 minutes.

4 Remove from heat and add the maple syrup, lemon juice, salt, and pepper. For a smoother dip, puree the mixture. Otherwise, leave chunky. Let the mixture cool.

5 When cool, place it in a small bowl and top with the tomato, if desired and parsley or cilantro. Sprinkle the dukkah on top and serve with pita chips.

Fried Okra

YIELD: 4 SERVINGS • ACTIVE TIME: 10 MINUTES
TOTAL TIME: 20 MINUTES

If you have reservations about trying a new food, there is a proven way to ease into it: fry it. Okra pairs very well with peppers of all kinds.

INGREDIENTS

½ lb. fresh okra, trimmed and cut into 2-inch pieces

Jane's Krazy Mixed-Up Salt, to taste

¼ cup cornmeal

¼ cup all-purpose flour

1 egg

Peanut oil, for frying

Salt, to taste

1 Spread the okra on a baking sheet and sprinkle them with the flavored salt.

2 Place the cornmeal and flour in a bowl and whisk to combine. In another bowl, beat the egg until scrambled.

3 Add peanut oil to a Dutch oven until it is 2 to 3 inches deep. Heat to 350°F over high heat.

4 Dip the chunks of okra in the egg, transfer to the cornmeal mixture, and toss to coat.

5 When the oil is hot enough that a crumb of cornmeal sizzles, add all of the okra that will fit and fry. Keep an eye on them, turning them gently as they brown. When brown on all sides (about 5 minutes), use a slotted spoon to remove them from the oil and place on a paper towel-lined plate. Let cool a few minutes and serve.

Pickled Okra

Okra pickles beautifully, and looks incredibly appealing in an appetizer spread.

1 In a large saucepan, bring 6 cups of water to a boil. This will serve as your bath once the jars have been filled.

2 Pack the okra, chilies, bay leaves, and garlic cloves into 2 sterilized 1-pint canning jars. Divide the dill seeds, coriander seeds, and peppercorns evenly between each jar.

3 In a medium saucepan, combine the water, vinegar, and salt and bring to a boil over high heat, stirring to dissolve the salt.

4 Pour the brine into the jars, leaving ½ inch of space free at the top. Apply the lids and bands.

5 Place the jars in the boiling water and boil for 10 minutes. Remove, let cool to room temperature, and serve immediately. These can be stored in a cool, dark place for up to 1 year. Refrigerate after opening.

INGREDIENTS

1 lb. okra, trimmed

4 small dried red chili peppers

2 bay leaves

2 garlic cloves, halved

1 teaspoon dill seeds

1 teaspoon coriander seeds

1 teaspoon black peppercorns

1½ cups water

1½ cups apple cider vinegar

1½ tablespoons kosher salt

Onion Rings

**YIELD: 4 SERVINGS • ACTIVE TIME: 15 MINUTES
TOTAL TIME: 20 MINUTES**

There's nothing like crispy onion rings. Pair with Creamy Adobo Dip for an extra treat!

INGREDIENTS

2 large yellow onions, sliced into thick rings

½ cup all-purpose flour

1 egg, beaten

⅓ cup whole milk

½ teaspoon paprika

½ cup plain bread crumbs

½ cup panko bread crumbs

1 tablespoon grated Parmesan cheese

Vegetable oil, for frying

Fine-grained salt, to taste

Creamy Adobo Dip (see recipe), for serving

For the Creamy Adobo Dip

2 tablespoons mayonnaise

2 tablespoons sour cream

1 teaspoon adobo sauce (from a can of chipotles in adobo sauce)

1 Place the flour in a shallow bowl, the beaten egg, milk, and paprika in another, and the bread crumbs and Parmesan in another.

2 Place a Dutch oven on the stove and add vegetable oil until it is 2 to 3 inches deep. Heat the oil until a few bread crumbs sizzle immediately when dropped in.

3 Dip the onion rings in the flour, then in the egg mixture, and lastly in the bread crumb mixture. Make sure the rings are fully covered by the bread crumb mixture. Carefully drop into the hot oil and fry for several minutes until brown.

4 Using tongs, turn over to brown the other side (if necessary) and then transfer to a paper towel-lined plate.

5 Sprinkle with fine-grained salt, let cool briefly, and serve with the Creamy Adobo Dip.

Creamy Adobo Dip

1 Place all of the ingredients in a bowl, stir to combine, and serve.

A stone-cold Canadian classic that the recent celebration of comfort food has ushered into the mainstream. The squeak provided by the cheese curds is just one of the many pleasures available in this dish.

1 Place the vegetable oil in a large cast-iron Dutch oven and heat to 275°F. Add the potatoes and fry for 5 minutes, while stirring occasionally. Use a slotted spoon to remove the potatoes, transfer to a paper towel-lined plate, and let them cool completely.

2 Heat the oil to 350°F. Add the cooled potatoes and fry until golden brown, about 5 minutes. Transfer to a paper towel-lined plate and sprinkle with salt.

3 Place the butter in a saucepan and warm over medium-high heat. When it is melted, add the flour and cook, while stirring, until the mixture is smooth, about 2 minutes.

4 Add the garlic and cook until soft, about 2 minutes. Stir in the stock, ketchup, vinegar, and Worcestershire sauce, season with salt and pepper, and bring to a boil. Cook, while stirring, until the gravy has thickened, about 6 minutes.

5 Remove from heat and pour gravy over each serving of fries. Top each with a handful of the cheese curds and serve immediately.

INGREDIENTS

4 cups vegetable oil

2 russet potatoes, cut into strips

Salt and pepper, to taste

4 tablespoons unsalted butter

¼ cup flour

1 garlic clove, minced

4 cups beef stock

2 tablespoons ketchup

1 tablespoon apple cider vinegar

½ tablespoon Worcestershire sauce

2 cups cheese curds

California Guacamole

YIELD: 2 CUPS • ACTIVE TIME: 10 MINUTES
TOTAL TIME: 10 MINUTES

Everyone should have a basic guacamole recipe on hand, as it is one of the finest things to do with an avocado. This recipe is a bona fide California classic.

INGREDIENTS

3 avocados, halved, seeded, and peeled

Juice of 2 to 3 limes, plus more for garnish

2 Roma tomatoes, seeded and diced

1 red onion, diced

1 to 2 garlic cloves, minced

½ teaspoon kosher salt

Black pepper, to taste

Old Bay seasoning, to taste

1 tablespoon chopped fresh cilantro, for garnish

1 Place the avocados in a small bowl and mash roughly.

2 Add lime juice, tomatoes, onions, garlic, salt, pepper, and Old Bay seasoning. Fold until everything is incorporated and the mixture has reached the desired consistency. While a chunkier guacamole is easier for dipping, pureeing the mixture in a food processor gives it a smoother finish.

3 Garnish with cilantro, top with a final splash of lime juice, and serve.

Beet Chips

YIELD: 4 TO 6 SERVINGS • ACTIVE TIME: 5 MINUTES
TOTAL TIME: 20 MINUTES

You may have tried a commercial brand of beet chips from the supermarket, but they are quite easy to make at home. In this recipe, you don't even have to enlist a deep fryer to get crispy, addictive chips.

1 Preheat the oven to 400°F. Place the beets and olive oil in a bowl and toss until the slices are evenly coated.

2 Place on a baking sheet in a single layer. Bake for 12 to 15 minutes, or until crispy.

3 Remove from the oven, transfer to a bowl, add the salt, and toss. Serve warm or store in an airtight container.

INGREDIENTS

5 beets, peeled and sliced very thin

¼ cup olive oil

2 teaspoons sea salt

Hot & Spicy Carrots

**YIELD: 4 SERVINGS • ACTIVE TIME: 15 MINUTES
TOTAL TIME: 1 HOUR AND 30 MINUTES**

This is a quick pickle recipe that can be used with other vegetables. You can marinate them for up to 5 days, but they will have plenty of flavor in just an hour.

INGREDIENTS

½ lb. daikon radish, peeled

½ lb. large carrots, peeled

1 cup unseasoned rice vinegar

1 teaspoon kosher or sea salt

2 tablespoons sugar, plus 2 teaspoons

1 cup water

1 Wash the daikon and carrots and cut into matchsticks or rounds that are about the size of a quarter. Pat dry.

2 Place the vinegar, salt, sugar, and water in a bowl and stir until the sugar dissolves. Add the carrots and daikon to the mixture and marinate for at least 1 hour before serving.

3 For the best flavor, store vegetables in an airtight mason jar in the refrigerator for up to 5 days.

INGREDIENTS

1 lb. fresh vegetables, such as cucumbers, carrots, green beans, summer squash, or cherry tomatoes

2 sprigs fresh herbs, such as thyme, dill, or rosemary (optional)

1 to 2 teaspoons whole spices, such as black peppercorns, coriander, or mustard seeds (optional)

1 teaspoon dried herbs or ground spices (optional)

2 garlic cloves, smashed or sliced (optional)

1 cup preferred vinegar

1 cup water

1 tablespoon kosher salt or 2 teaspoons pickling salt

1 tablespoon granulated sugar (optional)

Quick Pickles

YIELD: 2 PINTS • ACTIVE TIME: 15 MINUTES
TOTAL TIME: 12 HOURS TO 2 DAYS

This is a go-to recipe for pickles. It will produce classic cucumber pickles, but also works well for carrots, green beans, or cauliflower.

1 Wash two wide-mouth pint jars, lids, and bands in warm soapy water and rinse well. Set aside to dry or dry by hand.

2 Wash and dry the vegetables. Peel carrots, if using. Trim the ends of the green beans, if using. Cut vegetables into desired shapes and sizes.

3 Divide whatever herbs, spices, and/or garlic you are using between the jars.

4 Pack the vegetables into the jars, making sure there is ½ inch of space remaining at the top. Pack them in as tightly as you can without damaging the vegetables.

5 Combine the vinegar, water, and salt in a small saucepan and cook over high heat. If using, add the sugar. Bring to a boil, while stirring to dissolve the salt and sugar. Pour the brine over the vegetables, filling each jar to within ½ inch of the top. You may not use all the brine.

6 Gently tap the jars against the counter a few times to remove all the air bubbles. Top off with more pickling brine if necessary.

7 Place the lids on the jars and screw on the bands until tight.

8 Let the jars cool to room temperature. Store the pickles in the refrigerator. The pickles will improve with flavor as they age, so try to wait at least 2 days before serving.

Spicy Pickles

YIELD: 12 CUPS • ACTIVE TIME: 20 MINUTES
TOTAL TIME: 5 TO 8 HOURS

This is the perfect recipe to have on hand when cucumbers show up in the spring. With a little preparation, you can make sure you have enough of these delicious pickles to last all year.

INGREDIENTS

3 lbs. pickling cucumbers, sliced thin

3 small yellow onions, sliced thin

1 red bell pepper, stemmed, seeded, and sliced thin

2 habanero peppers, stemmed, seeded, and sliced thin

3 garlic cloves, sliced

3 cups sugar

3 cups apple cider vinegar

2 tablespoons mustard seeds

2 teaspoons turmeric

1 teaspoon black pepper

1/3 cup canning and pickling salt

1 Place the cucumbers, onions, peppers, and garlic in a large bowl.

2 Place the sugar, apple cider vinegar, mustard seeds, turmeric, and pepper in a large pot and bring to a boil over medium-high heat, stirring to dissolve the sugar.

3 Add the vegetables and the salt and return to a boil. Remove the pot from heat and let it cool slightly.

4 Fill sterilized mason jars with the vegetables and cover with the brine. Place the lids on the jars and secure the bands tightly. Place the jars in the boiling water for 40 minutes.

5 Use the tongs to remove the jars from the boiling water and let them cool. As they are cooling, you should hear the classic "ping and pop" sound of the lids creating a seal.

6 After 4 to 6 hours, check the lids. There should be no give in them, and they should be suctioned onto the jars. Discard any lids and food that did not seal properly.

Summer Vegetable Cheese Dip

YIELD: 4 TO 6 SERVINGS • ACTIVE TIME: 20 MINUTES
TOTAL TIME: 1 HOUR AND 45 MINUTES

This versatile dip is sure to be your go-to recipe. Its ability to accommodate leafy greens, slices of crusty bread, and almost any vegetable allows it to be used in any season.

INGREDIENTS

1 cup cream cheese or quark

½ cup sour cream

1 cup shredded mozzarella, plus more for topping

2 tablespoons fresh rosemary leaves

2 tablespoons fresh thyme leaves

½ cup diced summer squash

1 cup Swiss chard

1 cup spinach

6 garlic cloves, diced

2 teaspoons salt

1 teaspoon pepper

Slices of crusty bread, for serving

1 Place the cream cheese or quark, sour cream, and mozzarella in a bowl and stir until well combined.

2 Add the remaining ingredients for the dip, stir to combine, and place in the refrigerator for at least 1 hour.

3 Approximately 30 minutes before you are ready to serve the dip, preheat the oven to 350°F.

4 Transfer the dip to an oven-safe bowl, top with additional mozzarella, and bake until the cheese is melted and starting to brown, about 20 minutes. Remove from the oven and serve warm with slices of crusty bread.

TIP: QUARK IS A CREAMY, UNRIPE
CHEESE THAT IS POPULAR IN GERMANY
AND EASTERN EUROPEAN COUNTRIES.
IF YOU'RE INTRIGUED, CHECK OUT YOUR
LOCAL DAIRY FARM.

Black Bean Hummus

YIELD: 4 CUPS • ACTIVE TIME: 10 MINUTES
TOTAL TIME: 10 MINUTES

A new take on hummus that blends black beans with the usual suspects (tahini) plus a few unusual ones (anchovy paste). This flavorful dip works with crudité or warm pita bread.

INGREDIENTS

2 (14 oz.) cans black beans, plus more as needed

¼ cup tahini

¾ cup fresh lime juice

¾ cup olive oil

2 teaspoons sea salt

1 tablespoon black pepper

1 teaspoon Tabasco™

1 teaspoon anchovy paste

Water, as needed

Cilantro leaves, chopped, for garnish

Pita triangles, warmed, for serving

Crudité, for serving

1 Place all of the ingredients, except for those designated for garnish or for serving, in a food processor and blend until the desired consistency is achieved. If too thick, add a tablespoon of water. If too thin, add more black beans.

2 Place in the serving bowl, garnish with the cilantro, and serve with warm pita triangles and crudité.

Dilly Beans

YIELD: 5 PINTS • ACTIVE TIME: 10 MINUTES
TOTAL TIME: 1 WEEK

This is a classic preparation for green beans—perfect when they come in all at once in mid-summer.

1 Prepare a boiling water bath and 5 pint jars. Place lids and bands in a small saucepan and simmer over low heat while you prepare the beans.

2 Wash and trim the beans so that they will fit in the jars. If the beans are particularly long, cut them in half. Place the vinegar, water, and salt in a medium saucepan and bring to a boil.

3 While the pickling liquid heats, pack your beans into the jars, leaving ½ inch of space free at the top.

4 Place 1 clove of garlic, 1 teaspoon dill seeds, and 1 teaspoon red pepper flakes in each jar.

5 Slowly pour the hot brine over the beans, leaving ½ inch free at the top. After the jars are full, use a chopstick or butter knife to remove the air bubbles. Add more brine if necessary.

6 Wipe the rims, apply the lids and bands, and process in the hot water bath for 10 minutes. Let the beans sit for at least 1 week before serving.

INGREDIENTS

3 lbs. green beans

2½ cups white vinegar

2½ cups water

¼ cup pickling salt

5 garlic cloves

5 teaspoons dill seeds
(not dill weed)

5 teaspoons red pepper flakes

Jalapeño & Cheddar Cornbread

**YIELD: 12 SERVINGS • ACTIVE TIME: 15 MINUTES
TOTAL TIME: 55 MINUTES**

A simple batter with a burst of umami thanks to all that cheese. This will be somewhat spicy, so cut back on the jalapeños if you, or a loved one, prefer things mild.

INGREDIENTS

6 tablespoons unsalted butter

1 cup all-purpose flour

1 cup yellow cornmeal

½ cup sugar

1¾ teaspoons baking powder

1½ teaspoons baking soda

1 teaspoon kosher salt

2 large eggs, beaten

2 cups buttermilk

3 green jalapeño peppers, seeded and minced

2 oz. grated Cheddar cheese

2 oz. grated Monterey Jack cheese

1 Preheat the oven to 400°F.

2 Place the butter in a 10-inch skillet and place the pan in the oven as it warms.

3 Place the flour, cornmeal, sugar, baking powder, baking soda, and kosher salt in a mixing bowl and stir to combine. Add the eggs and buttermilk and beat with a large spoon until you have a thick batter.

4 Add the jalapeños and the cheeses and stir to evenly distribute.

5 Remove the skillet from the oven and pour the melted butter into the batter. Stir to combine then pour the batter back into the skillet.

6 Place in the oven and bake until puffy and golden brown, about 40 minutes. Let cool slightly before serving.

TIP: THIS CAN ALSO BE MADE IN A CORN STICK PAN OR MUFFIN PAN.

Salad with Charred Lemon Dressing

YIELD: 4 TO 6 SERVINGS • ACTIVE TIME: 20 MINUTES
TOTAL TIME: 30 MINUTES

Charring the lemons adds an intriguing bit of smoke to this terrific twist on a simple vinaigrette.

1 Place a large cast-iron skillet over high heat for 5 minutes.

2 Add the lemons to the skillet and let them char.

3 Transfer the lemons to a large strainer set over a bowl. Use a large spoon to crush the lemons and let the juice fall into the bowl. Discard the lemon peels and seeds.

4 Stir in the olive oil, salt, and pepper. Taste and season accordingly.

5 Place the remaining ingredients in a salad bowl and toss to combine. Add half of the dressing, toss to coat, and serve with the remaining dressing on the side.

INGREDIENTS

3 large lemons, quartered

1 cup olive oil

Salt and pepper, to taste

4 cups butter lettuce

6 radishes, sliced thin

2 tablespoons minced chives

¼ cup grated Parmesan cheese

Grilled Goat Cheese Appetizer

YIELD: 4 SERVINGS • ACTIVE TIME: 5 MINUTES
TOTAL TIME: 15 MINUTES

Without a doubt, the most famous chef in Argentina (and Uruguay) is Francis Mallmann. Renowned for his use of fire in cooking, he continually tries to return to and honor the most primal techniques while still elevating the ingredients. This recipe, which has been adapted to make indoors, remains a revelation. If you have the ability to make it over an open fire, try that as well. The additional smoke will be welcome.

INGREDIENTS

1 (8 oz.) log of goat cheese, sliced into 10 rounds

½ cup olive oil, plus 1 teaspoon

1 teaspoon red wine vinegar

1 cup dry, salt-cured black olives, pitted and chopped

¼ cup chopped walnuts

Large pinch of red pepper flakes, or to taste

2 teaspoons minced fresh oregano leaves

1 sourdough baguette, sliced and toasted

Salt and pepper, to taste

1 Arrange the goat cheese slices on a plate and place them in the freezer.

2 Place a cast-iron griddle or skillet over very high heat for 10 minutes.

3 Place the ½ cup of olive oil, red wine vinegar, olives, walnuts, red pepper flakes, and oregano in a bowl and stir to combine.

4 Lightly oil the griddle or skillet with the remaining olive oil. Place the cheese in a single layer and cook until brown and crusty on the bottom, about 2 minutes.

5 Use a spatula to remove the cheese and arrange the rounds on the toasted baguette slices. Spoon the olive mixture on top of the cheese, season with salt and pepper, and serve.

Kimchi

Simple and versatile, kimchi is the perfect introduction to all that fermentation has to offer.

INGREDIENTS

1 head Napa cabbage, cut into strips

½ cup kosher salt

2 tablespoons minced ginger

2 tablespoons minced garlic

1 teaspoon sugar

5 tablespoons red pepper flakes

3 bunches scallions, trimmed and sliced

Filtered water, as needed

1 Place the cabbage and salt in a large bowl and stir to combine. Work the mixture with your hands, squeezing to remove any liquid from the cabbage. Let the mixture rest for 2 hours.

2 Add the remaining ingredients, work the mixture until well combined, and squeeze to remove any liquid.

3 Transfer the mixture to a container and press down so it is tightly packed. The liquid should be covering the mixture. If it is not, add water until the mixture is covered.

4 Cover the jar and let the mixture sit at room temperature for 3 to 7 days, removing the lid daily to release the gas that has built up. When the taste is to your liking, store in an airtight container in the refrigerator.

Roasted Brussels Sprouts with Bacon, Blue Cheese & Pickled Red Onion

YIELD: 4 TO 6 SERVINGS • ACTIVE TIME: 15 MINUTES
TOTAL TIME: 50 MINUTES

Brussels sprouts have a bad reputation with a lot of folks, but when seared and seasoned well, their savory, nutty flavor is a revelation, able to go toe-to-toe with rich ingredients like bacon and blue cheese.

1 Place the vinegar, water, sugar, and salt in a saucepan and bring to a boil. Place the onion in a bowl and pour the boiling liquid over the slices. Cover and allow to cool completely.

2 Place the bacon in a large sauté pan and cook, stirring occasionally, over medium heat until crisp, about 7 minutes. Transfer to a paper towel–lined plate and leave the rendered fat in the pan.

3 Place the Brussels sprouts in the pan cut-side down, season with salt and pepper, and cook over medium heat until they are a deep golden brown, about 7 minutes.

4 Transfer the Brussels sprouts to a platter, top with the pickled onions, bacon, and blue cheese and serve.

INGREDIENTS

1 cup champagne vinegar

1 cup water

½ cup sugar

2 teaspoons kosher salt, plus more to taste

1 small red onion, sliced

½ lb. bacon, cut into 1-inch pieces

1½ lbs. Brussels sprouts, trimmed and halved

Black pepper, to taste

4 oz. blue cheese, crumbled

Basic Red Cabbage Slaw

**YIELD: 2 TO 4 SERVINGS • ACTIVE TIME: 10 MINUTES
TOTAL TIME: 2 TO 3 HOURS**

This is a topper that should be made a few hours ahead of time to give the cabbage time to soften. Once it is ready, it is a nice complement to grilled meats.

INGREDIENTS

1 small red cabbage, cored and sliced as thinly as possible

1 teaspoon kosher salt, plus more to taste

Juice of 1 lime

1 bunch fresh cilantro, chopped

1 Place the cabbage in a large bowl, sprinkle the salt on top, and toss to distribute. Use your hands to work the salt into the cabbage, then let it sit for 2 to 3 hours.

2 Once it has rested, taste to gauge the saltiness: if too salty, rinse under cold water and let drain; if just right, add the lime juice and cilantro, stir to combine, and serve.

Kohlrabi Slaw with Miso Dressing

YIELD: 4 SERVINGS • ACTIVE TIME: 10 MINUTES
TOTAL TIME: 10 MINUTES

The Asian flavors of this coleslaw are just perfect beside barbecue ribs. If you have a mandoline, it will make quick work of slicing the vegetables. A hand grater will also work.

INGREDIENTS

For the dressing

1 tablespoon white miso paste

1 tablespoon rice vinegar

1 teaspoon sesame oil

1 teaspoon peeled and minced fresh ginger

1 teaspoon soy sauce

3 tablespoons peanut oil

1 tablespoon sesame seeds

1 teaspoon maple syrup

For the coleslaw

3 kohlrabies, peeled and julienned or grated

2 carrots, peeled and julienned or grated

¼ cup minced fresh cilantro

¼ cup shelled pistachios, crushed

1 To prepare the dressing, place all of the ingredients in a mixing bowl and stir to combine. Set aside.

2 To begin preparations for the coleslaw, place the kohlrabies, carrots, and cilantro in a separate bowl and stir to combine.

3 Drizzle a few spoonfuls of the dressing into the coleslaw and stir until evenly coated. Taste, add more dressing if desired, top with the pistachios, and serve.

Sautéed Red Cabbage with Apples, Fennel & Balsamic

YIELD: 4 SERVINGS • ACTIVE TIME: 25 MINUTES
TOTAL TIME: 30 MINUTES

This is a lovely dish for fall when the weather cools.

1 Place the cabbage in a large sauté pan with a tablespoon of the butter and the water. Bring to a boil and cover the pan. Let the cabbage steam until the thick ribs are tender, 5 to 8 minutes, then remove the lid and cook until the water has evaporated.

2 Add the remaining butter, the apple, fennel seeds, and pinch of salt and pepper. Reduce heat to medium-low heat and cook, while stirring occasionally.

3 When the apples and cabbage have caramelized, add the balsamic vinegar, cook for another minute, and then serve with brown rice or mashed potatoes.

INGREDIENTS

½ red cabbage, cored and sliced

3 tablespoons unsalted butter

¼ cup water

1 apple, peeled, cored, and diced

1 teaspoon fennel seeds

Salt and pepper, to taste

1-2 tablespoons balsamic vinegar

Brown rice or mashed potatoes, for serving

Carrot Jicama Slaw

YIELD: 2 TO 4 SERVINGS • ACTIVE TIME: 5 MINUTES
TOTAL TIME: 5 MINUTES

Carrots and jicama are both sweet, so they need a zesty dressing. Fresh lime juice will give them some zip and the cilantro adds a citrusy flavor. If you can find toasted pumpkin seed oil, it really gives this slaw some backbone. If not, olive oil also works. Don't go in thinking the ancho chili powder is spicy, as it adds just a hint of smoke.

INGREDIENTS

½ lb. carrots, trimmed and peeled

½ lb. jicama, peeled

1-2 tablespoons fresh lime juice

1 tablespoons toasted pumpkin seed or olive oil

¼ teaspoon ancho chili powder

¼ cup chopped fresh cilantro

Salt, to taste

1 Grate the carrots and jicama into a bowl and stir to combine.

2 Add the remaining ingredients and gently toss to combine. Taste, adjust the seasoning as needed, and serve.

Grilled Corn with Chipotle Mayonnaise & Goat Cheese

YIELD: 4 SERVINGS • ACTIVE TIME: 10 MINUTES
TOTAL TIME: 45 MINUTES

The middle of summer, when the fresh corn hits the market, is the perfect time to make this dish. It's got it all—sweet corn, spice from the chipotle, and a soft, creamy landing thanks to the goat cheese.

INGREDIENTS

6 ears of corn

3 chipotle peppers in adobo

½ cup mayonnaise

¼ cup sour cream

1½ tablespoons brown sugar

1 tablespoon fresh lime juice

2 tablespoons chopped fresh cilantro, plus more for garnish

1 teaspoon kosher salt, plus more to taste

½ teaspoon black pepper, plus more to taste

3 tablespoons olive oil

½ cup crumbled goat cheese

6 lime wedges, for serving

1 Preheat the oven to 400°F.

2 Place the ears of corn on a baking sheet, place it in the oven, and bake for 25 minutes, until the kernels have a slight give to them. Remove from the oven and let cool. When the ears of corn are cool enough to handle, remove the husks and silk.

3 Preheat your gas or charcoal grill to 400°F. Place the chipotles, mayonnaise, sour cream, sugar, lime juice, cilantro, salt, and pepper in a food processor and puree until smooth. Set aside.

4 Drizzle the corn with olive oil, season with salt and pepper, and place on the grill. Cook, while turning, until they are charred all over.

5 Spread the mayonnaise on the corn, sprinkle the goat cheese on top, and garnish with additional cilantro. Serve with wedges of lime.

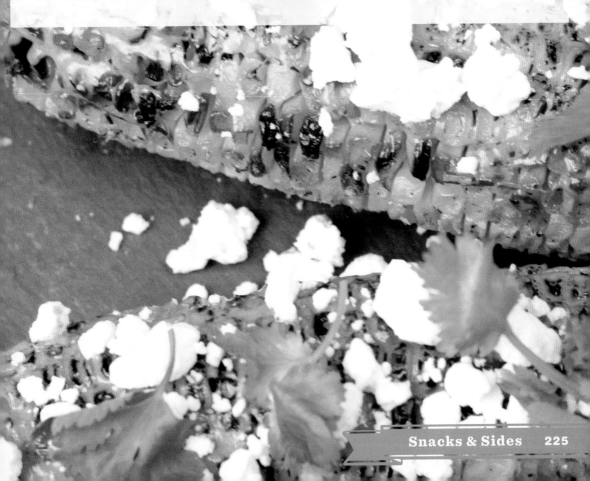

INGREDIENTS

6 strips thick-cut bacon

½ onion, diced

½ cup seeded and diced bell pepper

1 teaspoon kosher salt, plus more to taste

2 (14 oz.) cans pinto beans, rinsed and drained

1 cup barbecue sauce

1 teaspoon Dijon mustard

2 tablespoons dark brown sugar

Black pepper, to taste

Home-Style Baked Beans

YIELD: 6 TO 8 SERVINGS • ACTIVE TIME: 30 MINUTES
TOTAL TIME: 1½ TO 2 HOURS

Images of cowboys and campfires will be dancing in your head thanks to this cast-iron skillet version of baked beans.

1 Preheat the oven to 325°F.

2 Warm a 12-inch cast-iron skillet over medium heat and add half of the bacon pieces. Cook until it's just starting to crisp up, about 6 minutes. Transfer to a paper towel–lined plate.

3 Place the remaining bacon in the skillet, raise heat to medium-high, and cook, turning the bacon often, until they are browned and crispy, about 10 minutes. Reduce heat to medium. Add the onion and bell pepper and cook, stirring occasionally, until the vegetables start to soften, about 6 minutes.

4 Add the salt, beans, barbecue sauce, mustard, and brown sugar. Stir, season with additional salt and pepper, and bring to a simmer.

5 Lay the partially cooked pieces of bacon on top and transfer the skillet to the oven. Bake for 1 hour, until the bacon on top is crispy and browned, and the sauce is thick. If the consistency seems too thin, cook for an additional 15 to 30 minutes, checking frequently so as not to overcook the beans.

6 Remove from the oven and allow to cool slightly before serving.

Southern Collard Greens

YIELD: 4 TO 6 SERVINGS • ACTIVE TIME: 30 MINUTES
TOTAL TIME: 2 HOURS AND 30 MINUTES

Here's the thing about authentic Southern Collard Greens: when you think they are done, just keep cooking them.

INGREDIENTS

2 tablespoons olive oil

1 onion, diced

½ lb. smoked ham, diced

4 garlic cloves, diced

3 lbs. collard greens, stems removed, chopped

2 cups vegetable broth

¼ cup apple cider vinegar

1 tablespoon brown sugar

1 teaspoon red pepper flakes

1 Place the oil in a large saucepan over and warm over medium-high heat. When the oil starts to shimmer, add the onion and sauté until translucent, about 3 minutes. Add the ham, reduce heat to medium, and cook until the ham starts to brown, about 5 minutes.

2 Add the remaining ingredients, stir to combine, and cover the pan. Braise the collard greens until they are very tender, about 2 hours. Check on the collards every so often and add water if all of the liquid has evaporated.

Yu Choy with Garlic & Soy

**YIELD: 4 SERVINGS • ACTIVE TIME: 10 MINUTES
TOTAL TIME: 15 MINUTES**

Steaming yu choy keeps it tender and light. If the stalks are large, leave them to cook a little longer.

1 Put the yu choy in a sauté pan large enough to fit all of them, cover with the water, cover the pan, and cook over high heat.

2 After about 5 minutes, check the thickest stalk to see if it is tender. If not, cook until it is. Once tender, add the oil and the garlic. Sauté until the garlic is fully cooked but not browned, about 2 minutes.

3 Add the vinegar and soy sauce, toss to combine, and serve.

INGREDIENTS

1½ lbs. yu choy (if especially long, cut them in half)

¼ cup water

1 tablespoon olive oil

2 garlic cloves, chopped

½ tablespoon rice vinegar

1 tablespoon soy sauce

Confit New Potatoes

New potatoes are young potatoes that are pulled in early spring. They are sweeter than their mature counterparts, since the sugars haven't had time to develop into starches, and are so soft and tender that they don't need to be peeled.

INGREDIENTS

4 cups canola oil

5 lbs. new potatoes

Salt and pepper, to taste

1 Place the oil in a Dutch oven and bring it to 200°F over medium heat.

2 While the oil is warming, wash the potatoes and pat them dry. Carefully place the potatoes in the oil and cook until fork-tender, about 1 hour.

3 Drain the potatoes, season generously with salt and pepper, and stir to ensure that the potatoes are evenly coated. Serve immediately.

> **NOTE:** THESE POTATOES SHOULD HAVE PLENTY OF FLAVOR, BUT IF YOU'RE LOOKING TO TAKE THEM TO ANOTHER LEVEL, REPLACE THE CANOLA OIL WITH CHICKEN OR DUCK FAT.

INGREDIENTS

1½ lbs. low-starch, new or red potatoes, cubed

½ cup olive oil

3 tablespoons white wine vinegar

2 tablespoons dry white wine

1 teaspoon whole-grain Dijon mustard

1 teaspoon kosher salt, plus more to taste

1 shallot, minced

Black pepper, to taste

2 tablespoons chopped fresh parsley

2 tablespoons chopped fresh chives

2 tablespoons chopped fresh dill

Herbed Potato Salad

YIELD: 4 TO 6 SERVINGS • ACTIVE TIME: 10 MINUTES
TOTAL TIME: 25 MINUTES

The two most common potato salads have either a mayonnaise dressing or a sweet vinegar (German) dressing. The French have a different approach with shallots and herbs and a tangy vinaigrette that lets the natural sweetness of the potatoes come through. The dressing is poured on the potatoes when they are still warm, letting them soak up the flavor.

1 Add the potatoes to a pot of water large enough to hold them all, bring to a boil, reduce heat, and simmer until tender, about 15 minutes.

2 While the potatoes are simmering, whisk together the oil, vinegar, wine, mustard, and teaspoon of salt.

3 When the potatoes are done, drain them and place them in a bowl. Add the vinaigrette and shallot immediately and gently toss, making sure to coat all of the potatoes. Let cool completely.

4 Taste and adjust seasoning as needed. Add the black pepper and fresh herbs, stir to incorporate, and serve.

Mom's Creamed Spinach

YIELD: 4 SERVINGS • ACTIVE TIME: 20 MINUTES
TOTAL TIME: 25 MINUTES

This version of a comfort food staple is made with cream cheese and lots of onion. Definitely use frozen spinach for this one, especially if you are feeding a crowd.

INGREDIENTS

1 tablespoon unsalted butter

1 cup diced yellow onion

2 garlic cloves, chopped

1 lb. frozen chopped spinach

½ lb. cream cheese, at room temperature

Pinch of nutmeg

1 teaspoon marjoram

Salt and pepper, to taste

1 Place the butter in a wide sauté pan and melt over medium heat. Add the onion and garlic and cook until the onion is just translucent, about 3 minutes.

2 Add the frozen spinach to the pan along with a few teaspoons water, cover the pan, and cook for a minute. Remove the lid, break the spinach up, and cook until it is completely thawed.

3 Add the cream cheese, nutmeg, and marjoram and stir to incorporate. Cook until the sauce has reduced and thickened, about 5 minutes. Season with salt and pepper and serve.

Berbere Spice

1 teaspoon fenugreek

1 teaspoon red pepper flakes

2 tablespoons sweet paprika

½ teaspoon ground cardamom

1 teaspoon nutmeg

⅛ teaspoon garlic powder

⅛ teaspoon ground cloves

⅛ teaspoon cinnamon

⅛ teaspoon allspice

1 Use a mortar and pestle or spice grinder to combine all of the ingredients.

TIP: THIS CAN BE SERVED ON ITS OWN OR OVER QUINOA, MILLET, OR RICE.

Black-Eyed Peas with Coconut

YIELD: 4 SERVINGS • ACTIVE TIME: 10 MINUTES
TOTAL TIME: 1 HOUR AND 15 MINUTES

Black-eyed peas have a wonderful starchiness and nutty taste that is utilized far too infrequently. You can use canned peas in this preparation, but fresh will be better.

1 Drain the black-eyed peas, place them in a large, enameled cast-iron pot, and cover with water. Bring the water to a simmer and cook until the black-eyed peas are tender, about 45 minutes. Drain and set them aside.

2 Place the coconut oil in the large, enameled cast-iron pot and warm over medium heat. When the oil starts to shimmer, add the onion, tomatoes, habanero, and Berbere Spice and sauté for 2 minutes.

3 Add the coconut milk and stock and bring to a simmer. Reduce the heat to low and gently simmer until the liquid has slightly reduced, about 10 minutes.

4 Return the black-eyed peas to the pot and continue to simmer for 15 minutes.

5 Stir in the cilantro and serve immediately.

INGREDIENTS

1 cup dried black-eyed peas, soaked in cold water for 8 hours

4 tablespoons coconut oil

1 yellow onion, peeled and sliced

2 tomatoes, chopped

1 habanero pepper, stemmed, seeded, and chopped

2 teaspoons Berbere Spice (see recipe)

1 cup coconut milk

1 cup chicken stock

1 cup cilantro leaves, chopped

Puerto Rican Rice & Pigeon Beans

YIELD: 4 SERVINGS • ACTIVE TIME: 30 MINUTES
TOTAL TIME: 1 HOUR AND 10 MINUTES

The crusty layer of rice that results when you make the rice in a caldera is known as pegao, and, like all delicacies, getting it right is an art. So don't be discouraged if you get it wrong the first time, and know that getting it is well worth doing right. Serve this alongside pork ribs.

INGREDIENTS

4 cups long-grain white rice

2 oz. uncured bacon

1 tablespoon garlic powder

1 tablespoon onion powder

1 tablespoon ground cumin

1 teaspoon dried oregano

1 tablespoon ground achiote or turmeric

½ teaspoon ground black pepper

1 cup Sofrito (see recipe)

½ cup chopped yellow onion

1 tablespoon vegetable oil

2 tablespoons tomato paste

1 tablespoon capers

10 Spanish olives, chopped

1 (15 oz.) can of pigeon peas, drained

5 cups water

2 teaspoons kosher salt

1 Place the rice in a colander and rinse it three times to remove any starch. Set aside.

2 Place the bacon in a large, wide cast-iron caldera and cook it slowly over medium heat until it is very crispy, about 10 minutes. Transfer to a paper towel-lined plate. Leave the rendered fat in the pot. When the bacon is cool enough to handle, crumble it into bite-sized pieces.

3 Add the garlic powder, onion powder, cumin, oregano, achiote (or turmeric), and pepper to the pan and sauté for 20 seconds. Quickly add the Sofrito and onion, stir to combine, and cook for 3 minutes.

4 Add the rice and stir to combine. Cook for 3 minutes and then add the vegetable oil, the tomato paste, capers, olives, and pigeon peas. Stir gently to combine and cook, without stirring, for 1 or 2 minutes to allow the bottom layer of rice to stick to the bottom of the pan. If you do not want the crispy layer of rice, skip this step.

5 Add the water and salt and bring to a boil. Turn off the heat and quickly drape a clean kitchen towel over the pot. Place the lid on top and wrap the cloth up around the lid, making sure it does not hang down or it will catch fire. Turn the heat to high. Cook for 30 seconds and then reduce the heat to low. Simmer for 35 minutes.

6 After 35 minutes, raise the heat to high and wait 1 minute. Turn off the heat and let it steam for 5 minutes. Fluff with a fork, garnish with the crumbled bacon, and serve.

Sofrito

Zest and juice of 1 lime

Leaves from 1 large bunch of cilantro

INGREDIENTS

1 teaspoon dried oregano

1 red bell pepper, roasted and peeled

Large pinch of salt

½ yellow onion, chopped

6 garlic cloves

¼ cup olive oil

1 Place the ingredients in a blender and puree until smooth.

TIP: IF YOU CAN FIND THEM, ADD A BUNCH OF CULANTRO AND A CUBANELLE PEPPER TO THE BLENDER FOR A MORE AUTHENTIC SOFRITO.

Midsummer Corn & Bean Salad

**YIELD: 4 TO 6 SERVINGS • ACTIVE TIME: 15 MINUTES
TOTAL TIME: 24 HOURS**

This is a great make-ahead recipe when the local corn is ripe. In fact, if it is really fresh with great flavor, you can skip the cooking part altogether and use raw kernels. Dried beans bring the best flavor, but if you are pressed for time, use canned white or black beans. The maple syrup is meant to accentuate the sweetness of the corn, so add according to your personal preference.

INGREDIENTS

1 tablespoon olive oil

4 cups corn kernels (preferably fresh)

½ cup dried beans, soaked overnight

1 small red bell pepper, diced

1 small green bell pepper, diced

½ red onion, diced

Juice of ½ lime

1 teaspoon cumin

Tabasco™, to taste

3 tablespoons chopped fresh cilantro

1 tablespoon maple syrup, plus more to taste

Salt and pepper, to taste

1 Place the oil in a wide sauté pan, add the corn, and cook over medium-high heat until slightly brown, about 5 minutes. Remove from heat and let cool.

2 Drain the beans and place in a saucepan. Cover with water. Bring to a boil, reduce heat to a simmer, and cook until the beans are tender, about 45 minutes. Drain and cool.

3 Place all of the ingredients in a salad bowl, toss to combine, and chill in the refrigerator for 2 hours.

4 Taste, adjust seasoning as needed, and serve.

Cornbread with Honey

**YIELD: 16 SERVINGS • ACTIVE TIME: 40 MINUTES
TOTAL TIME: 2 HOURS AND 15 MINUTES**

Adding thick corn puree to a cornbread recipe adds a freshness straight cornmeal just can't approach.

INGREDIENTS

5 ears of corn

10 tablespoons unsalted butter

1 cup diced onion

1 tablespoon minced garlic

2½ tablespoons salt, plus more to taste

2¾ cups heavy cream

2 cups all-purpose flour

2 cups cornmeal

¼ cup brown sugar

2 tablespoons baking powder

½ teaspoon cayenne pepper

½ teaspoon paprika

1½ cups honey

6 eggs

¼ cup sour cream

1 Preheat the oven to 400°F.

2 Place the ears of corn on a baking sheet, place it in the oven, and bake for 25 minutes, until the kernels have a slight give to them. Remove from the oven and let cool. When the ears of corn are cool enough to handle, remove the husks and silk and cut the kernels from the cob. Reserve the corn cobs for another preparation. Lower the oven temperature to 300°F.

3 Place 2 tablespoons of the butter in a large saucepan and melt over medium heat. Add the onion and garlic, season with salt, and cook until the onion is translucent. Set ¾ cup of the corn kernels aside and add the rest to the pan. Add 2 cups of the cream and cook until the corn is very tender, about 15 to 20 minutes.

4 Strain, reserve the cream, and transfer the solids to the blender. Puree until smooth, adding the cream as needed if the mixture is too thick. Season to taste and allow the puree to cool completely.

5 Place the flour, cornmeal, 2½ tablespoons of salt, sugar, baking powder, cayenne pepper, and paprika in a large mixing bowl and stir until combined. Place 2 cups of the corn puree, the honey, eggs, remaining cream, and sour cream in a separate large mixing bowl and stir until combined. Gradually add the dry mixture to the wet mixture and whisk to combine. When all of the dry mixture has been incorporated, add the reserved corn kernels and fold the mixture until they are evenly distributed.

6 Grease an 11 x 7-inch baking pan and pour the batter into it. Place the pan in the oven and bake until a toothpick inserted into the center comes out clean, about 35 minutes. Remove from the oven and briefly cool before cutting.

Skillet Mac & Cheese

YIELD: 6 TO 8 SERVINGS • ACTIVE TIME: 30 MINUTES
TOTAL TIME: 1 HOUR

There's nothing like homemade macaroni and cheese, but it can get messy when you have to use several pots and pans to make and serve it. Here comes your cast-iron skillet to the rescue!

INGREDIENTS

1 lb. elbow macaroni or preferred pasta

1 tablespoon kosher salt

3 tablespoons unsalted butter, at room temperature

3½ tablespoons all-purpose flour

1½ cups whole milk, at room temperature or slightly warmed

¼ cup sour cream

¾ lb. sharp white cheddar cheese, grated

¼ lb. Gruyère cheese, grated

Salt and pepper, to taste

Dash of cayenne pepper

1 Preheat the oven to 425°F.

2 Put the macaroni in a 12-inch cast-iron skillet and add cold water so that it reaches 1½ inches below the top. Stir in the salt, turn heat to high, and cook the macaroni for about 10 minutes. Test a piece after about 7 minutes. The pasta should be al dente—nearly cooked through but still a bit chewy. When it is cooked, drain it in a colander over a large mixing bowl so the water is retained.

3 Put your skillet back on the stove over medium heat and add the butter. When it's melted, stir in the flour, with a wooden spoon if possible, to prevent lumps from forming. Once it starts to bubble, start to slowly add the milk, whisking constantly as you add it. Add about ½ cup at a time, being sure to whisk it in thoroughly before continuing. When all the milk is stirred in, let the sauce simmer over low heat until thickened, about 10 minutes.

4 Reduce the heat to medium-low and stir in the sour cream. When the mix is warm again, add the cheeses, stirring gently as they melt. Season with the salt, pepper, and cayenne.

5 Add the macaroni gently into the cheese sauce. If it seems too thick, add some of the reserved water. The consistency should be like a thick stew. When the noodles are hot, transfer the skillet to the oven.

6 Bake for about 15 minutes, then check. The dish should be bubbling and the cheese on top starting to brown. This takes somewhere between 15 and 25 minutes. Be careful not to let it burn. Let the macaroni cool slightly before serving.

Oyster Sliders with Red Pepper Mayonnaise

YIELD: 4 SERVINGS • ACTIVE TIME: 30 MINUTES
TOTAL TIME: 1 HOUR AND 15 MINUTES

The briny taste of the oysters pairs well with the sweetness of the King's Hawaiian Rolls for a crunchy between-meals snack that is sure to satisfy.

INGREDIENTS

3 red bell peppers

1 cup canola oil

1 cup cornmeal

Salt, to taste

½ lb. oyster meat

2 eggs, beaten

1 tablespoon unsalted butter

4 King's Hawaiian Rolls

½ cup mayonnaise

1 Preheat the oven to 400°F.

2 Place the red peppers on a baking sheet and bake, while turning occasionally, for 35 to 40 minutes, until they are blistered all over. Remove from the oven and let cool. When cool enough to handle, remove the skins and seeds and set the flesh aside.

3 Place the oil in a Dutch oven and bring it to 350°F over medium-high heat.

4 Place the cornmeal and salt in a bowl and stir to combine.

5 When the oil is ready, dip the oyster meat into the beaten eggs and the cornmeal-and-salt mixture. Repeat until evenly coated.

6 Place the oysters in the Dutch oven and fry until golden brown, about 3 to 5 minutes. Remove from the oil and set on a paper towel-lined plate to drain.

7 Place the butter in a skillet and melt over medium heat. Place the buns in the skillet and toast until lightly browned. Remove and set aside.

8 Place the roasted peppers and mayonnaise in a blender and puree until smooth. Spread the red pepper mayonnaise on the buns, add the fried oysters, and serve.

Metric Equivalents

Weights

1 ounce	28 grams
2 ounces	57 grams
4 ounces (¼ pound)	113 grams
8 ounces (½ pound)	227 grams
16 ounces (1 pound)	454 grams

Volume Measures

⅛ teaspoon		0.6 ml
¼ teaspoon		1.23 ml
½ teaspoon		2.5 ml
1 teaspoon		5 ml
1 tablespoon (3 teaspoons)	½ fluid ounce	15 ml
2 tablespoons	1 fluid ounce	29.5 ml
¼ cup (4 tablespoons)	2 fluid ounces	59 ml
⅓ cup (5⅓ tablespoons)	2.7 fluid ounces	80 ml
½ cup (8 tablespoons)	4 fluid ounces	120 ml
⅔ cup (10⅔ tablespoons)	5.4 fluid ounces	160 ml
¾ cup (12 tablespoons)	6 fluid ounces	180 ml
1 cup (16 tablespoons)	8 fluid ounces	240 ml

Temperature Equivalents

°F	°C	Gas Mark
225	110	¼
250	130	½
275	140	1
300	150	2
325	170	3
350	180	4
375	190	5
400	200	6
425	220	7
450	230	8
475	240	9
500	250	10

Length Measures

¹⁄₁₆-inch	1.6 mm
⅛-inch	3 mm
¼-inch	0.63 cm
½-inch	1.25 cm
¾-inch	2 cm
1-inch	2.5 cm

Index

ABOUT CIDER MILL PRESS BOOK PUBLISHERS

Good ideas ripen with time. From seed to harvest, Cider Mill Press brings fine reading, information, and entertainment together between the covers of its creatively crafted books. Our Cider Mill bears fruit twice a year, publishing a new crop of titles each spring and fall.

"Where Good Books Are Ready for Press"

Visit us online at
cidermillpress.com
or write to us at
PO Box 454
12 Spring St.
Kennebunkport, Maine 04046